MEASURING CUSTOMER
SATISFACTION

MEASURING CUSTOMER SATISFACTION

Development and Use
of Questionnaires

Bob E. Hayes

ASQC Quality Press
Milwaukee, Wisconsin

MEASURING CUSTOMER SATISFACTION
Development and Use of Questionnaires
Bob E. Hayes

Library of Congress Cataloging-in-Publication Data
Hayes, Bob E.
    Measuring customer satisfaction : development and use of
    questionnaires / Bob E. Hayes.
    p.   cm.
    Includes bibliographical references and index.
    ISBN 0–87389–131–7
    1. Consumer satisfaction. 2. Questionnaires.   I. Title.
HF5415.5.H385   1991
    658.8'12—dc20   91–28347
                                                    CIP

10 9 8 7 6

ISBN 0–87389–131–7

Acquisitions Editor: Jeanine L. Lau
Production Editor: Mary Beth Nilles
Set in Sabon by A-R Editions, Inc.
Cover and interior design by A-R Editions, Inc.
Printed and bound by BookCrafters

For a free copy of the ASQC Quality Press Publications Catalog,
including ASQC membership information, call 800-248-1946.

Printed in the United States of America

Printed on acid free recycled paper

ASQC
Quality Press
611 East Wisconsin Avenue
Milwaukee, Wisconsin 53202

To my daughter, Marissa.
She is the reason why I do the things I do.
I love you.
"Daddy can play now."

Contents

Preface

I wrote this book for two reasons. The first is related to the absence in the literature of discussions of customer satisfaction questionnaire development and use. Many authors have written books and articles about the importance of satisfying customers to successfully compete in today's business. These authors generally say that customer satisfaction is an important factor in determining the success of businesses and that customers' attitudes should be assessed. However, they neglect to show how such satisfaction measurements can be developed. A few authors have presented some material in the development of customer satisfaction questionnaires. These authors either have presented research concerning their own questionnaire (Zeithaml, Parasuraman, and Berry, 1990) or have reduced the topic of questionnaire development to one chapter (Cottle, 1990; Hanan and Karp, 1989), neglecting to discuss measurement issues related to questionnaire evaluation. In this book I present detailed information on developing customer satisfaction questionnaires that I hope will fill this void.

The second reason I wrote this book is related to my desire to present important scientific principles in simple, understandable terms. I present these scientific issues in relation to the development of customer satisfaction questionnaires, but these issues are equally applicable in an attempt to develop any attitude measure (e.g., employee attitude surveys). Although I do discuss several topics in scale development, my intent is not to cover the entire content of this area, but to present information directly related to the development of customer satisfaction questionnaires.

My approach in presenting these scientific principles is aided by many illustrations and diagrams of examples. They provide the reader a visual representation of the principles in the book. For instance, these examples are designed to facilitate the understanding of statistical analyses as well as scale development. I hope that including these examples will make the material easier to read.

The book contains five chapters. One chapter discusses the recent acceptance of the importance of customer satisfaction in the American economy, and the other four cover specific aspects of customer satisfaction questionnaire development and use. The chapters are designed to be complementary and to develop a coherent picture of customer satisfaction questionnaire development and use. In addition, several appendices present important statistical concepts to aid readers who lack a statistical background. An understanding of the information in the appendices, however, is not essential to developing customer satisfaction questionnaires.

Chapter 1 introduces the concept of quality and emphasizes the importance of assessing customer satisfaction. Awareness of the importance of customer satisfaction stems from two sources: 1) a national quality award given to outstanding American companies who demonstrate product and service quality; and 2) the desire to achieve financial security of companies which are able to satisfy their customers and subsequently able to keep them. In addition, this chapter presents a model designed as an overview for the remaining chapters. This model will allow the reader to see the big picture of customer satisfaction questionnaire development and use before reading about the specific steps in subsequent chapters.

Chapter 2 covers two methods of determining important service or product characteristics as perceived by the customer. These methods are called the quality dimension development process and the critical incident technique. The quality dimensions include those general aspects of the service or product that customers say define the quality of the service or product. The two methods also identify specific examples of these important characteristics which will help determine the types of questions to be included in a customer satisfaction questionnaire.

It is important to evaluate the quality of any measurement system. When we measure parts that come from an assembly line, we want to be sure that the measurement process accurately reflects the true size of the parts we are measuring. Similarly, we want to ensure that the measurement of our customers' attitudes accurately reflects their attitudes. Imprecise measurement can lead to poor business decisions. Chapter 3 covers measurement issues related to customer satisfaction questionnaires, discusses issues of reliability and validity, and contains formulae to estimate reliability.

Chapter 4 presents guidelines for developing questionnaires: types of questions to be included, characteristics of good questions, response formats, and information to be included in the introduction.

Chapter 5 includes five examples of customer satisfaction questionnaires. The first three involve the manufacturing industry, the service industry, and the software industry. The latter two cover support functions within an organization: an internal statistical support group and a facilities group. This chapter discusses methods of presenting the data and suggests specific uses, including identifying which aspects of the service or product are especially important in customer satisfaction. In addition, this chapter applies customer satisfaction questionnaires to the traditional quality improvement techniques of control charting and describes their use in conducting organizational comparisons.

Several appendices are included as well. Each covers a specific topic related to statistical analysis. These appendices aim to help the lay reader understand key statistical concepts that complement the materials presented in the main body of the book. These appendices present a very general overview. Topics include measurement scales, frequencies, descriptive statistics, sampling error, the concept of hypothesis testing, and formal hypothesis testing procedures (t-tests, analysis of variance, and regression analysis).

I would like to thank some people who have helped me in various capacities with this book. Many of my friends and relatives reviewed earlier drafts of the book and provided the resources necessary to complete it. I would like to thank Tom Hayes for reading the first version of this book. His insights on presenting the information in chapter 3 were invaluable. Thanks "Boing-chang."

Also, I would like to thank Lamona Foster for her help in reviewing and editing my work. Her contribution made the book "uncategorically" better. Rosanne Holdaway-Brennan read the entire manuscript and provided excellent advice for the "continuous quality improvement strategy for team players in satisfying their customers." Karen Barbera, Rob Schmieder, and Deb Schroeder provided technical insight for the measurement chapter. Only critical reviews provide a means for improvement; these reviewers were extremely critical. Thank you for editing my work. I will never again let you read anything I write. I would like to thank Ann Brian and Deb Schroeder for providing the facilities I needed to complete this book. Special thanks are extended to Crystal Inman at The Ultimate. Also, I would like to thank Leah Rewolinski who edited this book. I think she did an outstanding job.

My family has always been there when I needed them. I think about them often, even though the fact that I forget their birthdays (except for my twin brother's) might indicate otherwise. I would like to thank them for the encouragement and support they have given me throughout the project, and throughout my life. I apologize for missing your birthdays.

One

INTRODUCTION

There has been an increase in the emphasis on a company's ability to produce high-quality products and/or provide high-quality services. In fact, many companies, in their attempt to compete in the marketplace, form either an organization to address various quality-related issues for the entire company or quality-improvement teams to address specific quality-related problems. Not only do companies rely on their own employees for quality improvement, they also rely on consultants who specialize in quality improvement techniques and methodologies. The primary goal of these specialists is to increase the quality of the products and services of the companies they serve.

To increase the quality of products and services, we first need to define quality. I will use the definition presented by Montgomery (1985): Quality is the extent to which products meet the requirements of people who use them. He further distinguishes between two types of quality: quality of design and quality of conformance.

Quality of design reflects the extent to which a product or service possesses an intended feature. For example, an automobile with power steering, a sun roof, and many other luxury options would be considered to have better quality of design than a car without these options. Quality of conformance reflects the extent to which the product or service conforms to the intent of the design.

These aspects of quality can be measured. Such measures give businesses an accurate indication of the "well-being" of their business processes and determine the quality of products and services resulting from these processes. Measures allow a business to: 1) know how well the business process is working; 2) know where to make changes to create improvements, if changes are needed; and 3) determine if the changes led to improvements. Various measurement techniques can index the quality of business processes, products, and services. Measures of quality often focus on objective or *hard* indices. For example, in manufacturing industries, the process of producing parts is conducive to measurements of size (e.g., of parts) and amount (e.g., of scrap or rework). In non-manufacturing industries, measurements could include time to complete a service or number of written errors on a particular form.

Recently, however, there has been a desire to utilize more subjective or *soft* measures as indicators of quality. These measures are *soft* because they focus on perceptions and attitudes rather than more concrete, objective criteria. It is often necessary to use these measures because objective indices are not applicable in assessing the quality of services. Also, companies are simply interested in gaining a more comprehensive understanding of their customers' perceptions. These *soft* measures include customer satisfaction questionnaires to determine customers' perceptions and attitudes concerning the quality of the service or product they received, as well as employee attitude questionaires that assess employees' perceptions about the quality of their work life.

Measurement of customers' attitudes is becoming an important element in the quality movement of American organizations. For instance, the Malcolm Baldrige National Quality Award (1990), given annually to American companies which demonstrate high standards of business practice, includes seven criteria or categories on which companies are judged. Of these seven categories, the most highly weighted is "customer satisfaction." Within this category, companies are judged on their knowledge of customer requirements and expectations (Category 7.1), their determination of customer satisfaction (Category 7.6), their ability to summarize satisfaction results (Category 7.7), and the results of comparisons to other companies (Category 7.8).

Knowledge of customers' perceptions and attitudes about an organization's business will greatly enhance its opportunity to make better business decisions. These organizations will know their customers' requirements or expectations and will be able to determine if they are meeting those requirements. To use customers' perceptions and attitudes to assess the quality of products and services, customer satisfaction instruments must accurately measure these perceptions and attitudes. If the instruments are poorly developed and inaccurately represent customers' opinions, decisions based on this information can be detrimental to the success of the organization. On the other hand, organizations with accurate information about customers' perceptions about the quality of the service and product can make better decisions to better serve their customers.

The combination of a competitive marketplace and the Malcolm Baldrige National Quality Award has heightened the awareness of American companies of the need to focus their quality improvement efforts on customer-related issues. To incorporate customers' perceptions and attitudes into their quality improvement efforts, companies must be able to gauge customers' attitudes accurately. One way to measure customers' attitudes is through questionnaires. These companies should design customer satisfaction questionnaires that accurately assess customers' perceptions about the quality of service or product.

The purpose of this book is to outline some guidelines which will aid in the development of customer satisfaction questionnaires. In addition, this book contains specific examples applying these guidelines. These guidelines are based on information combining both practical standards and scientific standards (AERA, APA & NCME, 1985). This book is written for professional practitioners in quality-related or marketing fields which can use customer attitude measurements. In addition, companies with quality improvement programs will find this book useful in developing measures to assess their clientele's level of satisfaction.

It should be mentioned that the use of customer satisfaction questionnaires seems most appropriate for organizations in the service sector or other non-manufacturing fields. Unlike the manufacturing industry, in which quality can be assessed by an objective index like the size of produced parts, the service sector offers little in the way of objective quality measures. Even *hard* measures (e.g., time) used in the non-manufacturing environment might not reflect the true quality of the service. For example, if the transaction completion time for a service is measured by a stopwatch and indicates a fast completion time, this does not ensure that customers perceive the completion time as fast. The customer may have expected an even faster time. Because quality is determined, in part, by the extent to which goods meet the customers' requirements, the measurement of quality in non-manufacturing settings is probably best indexed by customers' perceptions of the service they received.

Due to the differences in the output between manufacturing and non-manufacturing companies, customer satisfaction questionnaires will more likely find greatest use in non-manufacturing settings. However, questionnaires can still be applied in manufacturing environments. For example, although the quality of manufactured products is assessed by objective indices (in fact, automobiles are rated in *Consumer Reports* by objective indices such as number of repairs), automobile manufacturers are using the term "customer satisfaction" to advertise their automobiles. Some automobile manufacturers claim they are designing their cars to make the driver feel better. Although customers' perception of quality is probably correlated with objective indices of quality, automobile companies that make statements concerning customers' perceptions about their car can and should use customer satisfaction measures to assess the customers' perception about the quality of their cars.

Therefore, customer satisfaction questionnaires can be used in both non-manufacturing and manufacturing fields. The use of customer satisfaction questionnaires offers companies another approach in the assessment of the quality of their goods. It focuses an organization's attention on the customers and how they perceive the organization's products and services.

The entire American economy seems to be revolving around the phrase "customer satisfaction." There is a strong desire to establish and use measures of customers' attitudes as indices of the company's quality. Often, this desire stems from the lack of quality measures available to some companies (especially service companies) or results from an interest in satisfying customers. This desire to measure customers' attitudes should be paralleled by the knowledge of customer satisfaction questionnaire development. To enable companies to assess their customers' attitudes, technical guidelines on the development of customer satisfaction questionnaires must keep pace with this ever-increasing emphasis on customer satisfaction issues. The following chapters contain guidance on an appropriate method for developing and using questionnaires.

MODEL OF CUSTOMER SATISFACTION
QUESTIONNAIRE DEVELOPMENT AND USE

As an introduction to the remainder of the book, I would like to present a model describing the development and use of customer satisfaction questionnaires. This model appears in Figure 1.1 and illustrates the process in general. Each phase of the process contains specific steps, each focusing on an important element in the understanding of customers' opinions. As you read the book, it might be beneficial to keep this model in mind. It will help you incorporate the details of each chapter into a "big picture." This model also allows you to see how different parts of each chapter are interrelated.

Step 1 in the process is identifying customers' requirements or quality dimensions, the important characteristics of a product or service. Customer requirements define the quality of your products or services. In this step, not only do you identify the quality dimensions, you also identify specific examples of these dimensions.

Knowledge of customer requirements is essential for two reasons. First, it provides a better understanding of the way your customers define the quality of your services and products. If you understand customer requirements, you are in a better position to know how to satisfy your customers. Second, knowledge of customer requirements will facilitate the development of the customer satisfaction questionnaire. Its questions should assess the extent to which customers are satisfied on each of the quality dimensions. Chapter 2 includes information on identifying the customer requirements.

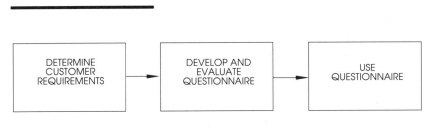

FIGURE 1.1 A general model for the development and use of customer satisfaction questionnaires

Step 2 in the process is developing the questionnaire. This step includes many specific components. The ultimate goal of this step is to develop a questionnaire that allows the assessment of specific information about your customers' perceptions. The specific information should correspond to the underlying customer requirements you identified in Step 1. Chapter 3 includes information concerning the evaluation of questionnaires. Chapter 4 covers the development of the questionnaire, including the selection of questions for the questionnaire (characteristics of good items), the choice of response formats, and the method of selecting the best items to be included in the questionnaire.

Once the questionnaire has been developed, the next step is to use it. Step 3 represents the many specific uses of customer satisfaction questionnaires. Each use allows you to obtain specific information about your customers' perceptions. The uses vary from identifying the current status of customer satisfaction to assessing customer satisfaction over time. Chapter 5 includes some specific uses of customer satisfaction questionnaires.

Tables at the end of chapters 2, 4, and 5 summarize the text of each chapter. These tables provide practical guides and a general outline in the development and use of customer satisfaction questionnaires; consult the text to obtain the exact procedures involved at each general step.

Two

DETERMINING CUSTOMER REQUIREMENTS

We usually describe a product or service in terms of several dimensions or characteristics. For example, after receiving a service, we might describe the service provider as fast, always available when needed, and unpleasant. These descriptions represent three different aspects of the service: *responsiveness*, *availability*, and *professionalism*, respectively. These are a subset of all possible dimensions by which the service can be described. The composite of all possible dimensions describes the entire product or service.

We can regard customer requirements as those characteristics of the product or service which represent important dimensions. They are the dimensions on which customers base their opinion about the product or service. I will use the term "quality dimensions" to describe these important dimensions. Also, I will interchange the terms "customer requirements" and "quality dimensions" throughout the book.

The purpose of determining customer requirements is to establish a comprehensive list of all the important quality dimensions that describe the service or product. It is important to understand the quality dimensions so that you will know how customers define the quality of your service or product. Only by understanding the quality dimensions will you be able to develop measures to assess these quality dimensions.

Although there may be some standard quality dimensions that generalize across many products or services, some dimensions will apply only to specific types of products or services. Quality dimensions applicable to many service organizations include *availability*, *responsiveness*, *convenience*, and *timeliness* (Kennedy and Young, 1989). These quality dimensions seem applicable to many service industries, such as the banking, hotel, and hospital industries. This list of quality dimensions, however, is not comprehensive for each of these industries. The hospital industry might include additional quality dimensions such as *quality of food* and *quality of care*. Similarly, other industries may possess quality dimensions that uniquely define their services and products. It is important that each company identify all quality dimensions to ensure understanding of the definition of quality for its products or services. Analyzing the services or products will provide a comprehensive picture of these dimensions.

This chapter will present two methods designed to identify important quality dimensions of products or services. The first method is the quality dimension development approach. This approach calls for the provider to establish the quality dimensions of its service or product. The second method is the critical incident approach (Flanagan, 1954) and involves customers in determining the quality dimensions.

QUALITY DIMENSION DEVELOPMENT

This method involves the people who provide the service or product. They should be in a good position to understand the purpose and function of the service or product. These people could range from individuals within a quality circle addressing a particular problem to individuals working independently to better understand their customers' requirements. In either case, these people are closely involved with the business process. Essentially, this process involves two steps: 1) identifying the dimensions; and 2) defining these dimensions with specific examples.

Identification of quality dimensions

The first step involves identifying the dimensions that define the quality of the service or product. This list of dimensions can be generated in various ways, using different sources of information. One way is to investigate literature (such as scientific, professional, and trade journals) that discusses specific industries. These publications might provide dimensions of the service or product.

As an example of information found in scientific journals, researchers (Parasuraman, Zeithaml, and Berry, 1985) have concluded that service quality can be described on the basis of 10 dimensions. Attempts to measure these 10 dimensions, however, reveal that customers can only distinguish between five dimensions (Parasuraman, Zeithaml, and Berry, 1988), suggesting that the original 10 dimensions overlap each other considerably. The five dimensions of service quality are tangibles, reliability, responsiveness, assurance, and empathy. Definitions of these dimensions are available in a recent publication on service quality by Zeithaml, Parasuraman, and Berry (1990).

Some trade journals often include articles that pertain to a particular industry. For example, various quality dimensions of staff support areas were presented by Kennedy and Young (1989). Five dimensions of staff support and their definitions appear in Table 2.1. These quality dimensions were identified as important characteristics of staff support areas.

Both of these examples demonstrate the usefulness of examining journals to obtain information for establishing a list of quality dimensions. By reading journals, you can gain insight from many knowledgeable people who have extensive experience in a particular field. Journals, either scientific or trade, provide an excellent resource for identifying quality dimensions.

Another way to establish a list of quality dimensions is to study the service or product. This study should include people involved in the business process. These people are in a good position to understand the purpose or function of their job in relation to meeting customers' expectations. This examination of the service or product should lead to a list of many dimensions.

Some dimensions might include those found in Table 2.1, or, again, the dimensions might be specific to a particular industry or organization. The initial list of dimensions will be in general terms such as *timely* or *professional*. These terms are to be used as guides toward understanding the dimensions of the service or product. Each term represents a particular quality dimension or customer requirement.

1. *availability of support:* the degree to which the customer can contact the provider

2. *responsiveness of support:* the degree to which the provider reacts promptly to the customer

3. *timeliness of support:* the degree to which the job is accomplished within the customer's stated time frame and/or within the negotiated time frame

4. *completeness of support:* the degree to which the total job is finished

5. *pleasantness of support:* the degree to which the provider uses suitable professional behavior and manners while working with the customer

TABLE 2.1 Some quality dimensions for staff support areas and their definitions

It is important to define these terms so that someone reading the definitions will understand precisely what is meant by each dimension. To clarify the definitions of the quality dimensions further, write specific examples for each quality dimension. This process is presented below.

Establishing specific examples of quality dimensions

The process of clarifying the quality dimensions is one of generating specific examples of the quality dimensions. Each example defines a particular quality dimension, and each dimension could include multiple examples. These examples are specific declarative statements, each describing a specific instance of the quality dimension it represents. The statements could be a specific task or behavior performed by a person within the process, or could describe a specific example illustrating the dimension. The former type of statement should include an action verb describing a specific behavior of the service provider or product. The latter statement should include a specific adjective reflecting the content of the dimensions. Example statements that contain both specific behavior and specific adjectives are included in Table 2.2. These statements were generated by the author using definitions presented by Kennedy and Young (1989).

These statements should reflect instances of performance by the staff or product which customers can assess. It is important that your list includes all possible examples for a particular dimension. This list of examples reflects the content of the dimensions, so if the list is deficient, a complete understanding of each dimension will also be deficient. You should try to include at least four or five statements for each dimension. After generating the list of statements, you may take the additional step of combining some quality dimensions that seem redundant. Some of the statements may overlap considerably and may not warrant separate dimensions.

The two steps in this process (generating dimensions and developing specific examples), although presented as independent of each other, are sometimes done simultaneously. Also, sometimes you may first generate specific examples which, in turn, lead to the generation of customer requirements. In either case, it is important that quality dimensions be defined by specific examples. Ultimately, the quality dimension development process will result in a list of customer requirements or quality dimensions, each defined by specific statements. The following example illustrates the process and outcome of the quality dimension development process. The example involves the software industry.

Availability of support

1. I could get help from the staff when I needed.
2. The staff was always available to help.
3. I could contact the staff at any time I needed.
4. The staff was there when needed.
5. I could arrange convenient meeting times with the staff.

Responsiveness of support

1. They were quick to respond when I asked for help.
2. They immediately helped me when I needed.
3. I waited a short period of time to get help after I asked for it.

Timeliness of support

1. They completed the job when expected.
2. They met my deadline(s).
3. They finished their responsibilities within the stated time frame.
4. The project was completed on time.

Completeness of support

1. They ensured that every aspect of the job was completed.
2. They completed everything they said they would do.
3. They were there to provide help from the beginning to the end of the project.

Professionalism of support

1. The staff members conducted themselves in a professional manner.
2. The staff listened to me.
3. The staff was courteous.
4. The staff cared about what I had to say.

Overall satisfaction with support

1. The quality of the way the staff treated me was high.
2. The way the staff treated me met my needs.
3. The way the staff treated me met my expectations.
4. I am happy with the way the staff treated me.
5. I am satisfied with the way the staff treated me.

Overall satisfaction with product

1. The quality of the final job they provided was high.
2. The job met my expectations.
3. I am satisfied with the job the staff provided.

TABLE 2.2 Declarative statements describing the quality dimensions of staff support areas

Software industry

In a recent article Murine (1988) discussed the measurement of software quality and listed 13 software quality factors. These factors are user-oriented and can be evaluated by the customer. I have extracted the dimensions and their definitions directly from the article and have written statements to provide specific examples of each dimension. The dimension, a brief definition, and the specific statements are presented in Table 2.3. These specific statements are only a small portion of the possible statements that could have been generated. Other questionnaire developers, examining the same quality dimensions, could generate more statements similar in content to the ones presented here.

Summary

Quality dimension development is a process of identifying customer requirements through various sources. One source is published literature covering specific industries that might contain information concerning some quality dimensions or customer requirements. Another potential source involves asking people within the company to examine the business process and determine the key quality dimensions of the service or product they provide. In addition to determining these dimensions, you should generate specific examples illustrating exactly what is meant by the dimensions. This process will lead to the development of a list of customer requirements, each defined by several specific statements.

CRITICAL INCIDENT APPROACH

The critical incident technique (Flanagan, 1954) is another approach for determining customer requirements. It has been used in establishing performance dimensions in performance appraisal systems (Latham, Fay, and Saari, 1979; Latham and Wexley, 1977). This method is not only applicable in developing customer satisfaction questionnaires but is equally valuable in any business process analysis in which companies attempt to define and understand their customers' requirements. The present method can greatly facilitate this process of definition and understanding.

The critical incident approach focuses on obtaining information from customers about the services and products they receive. "Customers" is a generic term referring to anybody who receives a service or product from some other person or group of people. It is clear that various customer

I.   Correctness: the degree to which the software meets customers' specifications
  1. I am able to complete my job with this software.
  2. The software meets my specifications in getting my job done.

II.   Reliability: the extent to which programs perform intended functions with precision
  3. I am able to perform functions with precision.
  4. The software allows me to perform functions accurately.

III.   Usability: effort required to understand output from programs
  5. I was able to learn about the output from programs in a short amount of time.
  6. The output of the programs is easy to understand.

IV.   Maintainability: effort required to find and correct an error in operational programs
  7. Locating an error in the operational program is easy.
  8. Fixing an error in the operational program is easy.

V.   Testability: effort required to test programs to ensure they perform intended function
  9. The testing of the program required a short amount of time.
  10. Testing the program to ensure it performed functions was easy.

VI.   Portability: effort required to transfer programs between hardware configurations and/or software environments
  11. Transferring the program between different hardware configurations is easy.
  12. I am able to transfer programs between different software environments with little problem.

VII.   Interoperability: effort required to couple one system to another
  13. Coupling one system to another is easy.
  14. The software allows for simple coupling between systems.

VIII.   Intra-operability: effort required to communicate between software components
  15. Communicating between software components is simple.
  16. I am able to communicate between software components easily.

IX.   Flexibility: effort required to modify operational programs
  17. I am able to modify the operational program with little effort.
  18. Changing the operational program is easy.

Overall satisfaction:
  19. I am very happy with the software.
  20. The software meets my expections.

TABLE 2.3 Quality dimensions, their definitions, and statements for the software industry

satisfaction questionnaires can be developed for different types of customers and that "customers" can be people who are external to an organization or people from a different department within the same organization. In either case, the critical incident approach can identify customer
requirements.

The strength of the critical incident approach lies in its utilization of
customers in defining customer requirements. Customers are in a good
position to help you understand these requirements because they are the
recipients of your services or products. Relying solely on organization or
department standards in determining customer requirements might lead
to a poor list which does not include factors important to customers.
Also, such a list may reflect customer requirements that should not be
included. The critical incident approach identifies specific performance
examples that illustrate organizational performance related to the services or products which they provide.

Critical incidents

A "critical incident" is an example of organizational performance from
the customers' perspective. That is, critical incidents are those aspects of
organizational performance which customers come in contact directly.
As a result, these incidents usually define staff performance (in service
organizations) and product quality (in manufacturing organizations).

A critical incident is a specific example of the service or product that
describes either positive or negative performance. A positive example is a
characteristic of the service or product that the customer would like to
see every time he/she receives that service or product. A negative
example is a characteristic of the service or product which would make
the customer question the quality of the company.

A good critical incident for defining customer requirements has two
characteristics: 1) it is *specific*; and 2) it describes the service provider in
behavioral terms or describes the service or product with *specific adjectives*. These characteristics should be explained to those responsible for
generating the critical incidents.

A critical incident is *specific* if it describes a single behavior or characteristic of the service or a single characteristic of the product. The incident should be written so that it is interpreted the same way by different
people. The critical incident is not specific if it describes several aspects
of performance. For example, a bad specific critical incident might say:

> I went to the bank to cash a check and waited in line for a long time.
> While I was waiting, I noticed that the teller was quickly servicing
> her customers.

This critical incident is not specific because it describes two different incidents. The reader would not know whether to focus on the fact that the customer waited a long time or that the teller was quick in the service she provided. Examples of good critical incidents would be to divide the previous example into two separate incidents:

1. I waited in line for a long time.

2. The teller was quickly servicing her customers.

A critical incident should also focus on behaviors of the service provider or specific adjectives that describe the service or product. An incident such as "the teller was not able to help me" does not specify what the teller did and why the teller was unable to help. Good incidents are:

1. The teller carefully listened to my request.

2. I received immediate service for my transaction.

The first critical incident describes a behavior of the teller while the second incident uses a specific adjective to describe the service.

GENERATING CRITICAL INCIDENTS

This procedure involves two steps. In the first, customers are interviewed to obtain specific information about the service or product. In the second, this information is categorized into groups, each group reflecting a quality dimension. A detailed discussion of both steps follows.

Interview

There are two approaches for obtaining critical incidents: group interviewing and individual interviewing. The major difference is that either groups or individuals are the focus of the generating process. A minor difference is that individual interviews can be conducted either in person or over the telephone. In either group or individual interviewing, the method of generating critical incidents is the same, and the following procedure is equally applicable.

For the first step, it is essential that you obtain the input of people who have received the service or product. These people must be actual customers who have had several interactions with the service provider or the product, since they will be providing specific examples of service or product quality.

The recommended number of customers to be interviewed ranges from 10 to 20 people. This high number of interviewees is recommended so that the possibility of deficient information from one interviewee will be offset by sufficient information from another interviewee. Thus, information obtained from the interviews will more likely completely cover the spectrum of customer requirements. Also, if group interviews are conducted, critical incidents stated by one person may stimulate incidents from other group members.

The interviewer should ask each interviewee to describe 5 to 10 positive instances and 5 to 10 negative instances of that service or product they received in the past. These positive and negative instances constitute the critical incidents that define good and poor service or product quality.

Recall that the interviewee should avoid using general terms to describe critical incidents. If the interviewee uses general phrases such as "the service was nice" or "the product was good," the interviewer should determine what the merchant actually did, in behavioral terms, that made him/her "nice," or which aspects of the product made it "good."

For example, two critical incidents a customer could provide are "The merchant was quick to respond when I arrived" and "The merchant was good." The latter critical incident does not specify why the merchant was good. The former critical incident specifically describes why the merchant was nice: the merchant was quick in responding to the customer. By pressing the interviewees to supply specific examples of performance or specific adjectives of the service or product, the interviewer obtains critical incidents which more efficiently define customer requirements. In addition, specific critical incidents will facilitate the development of the customer satisfaction questionnaire.

Categorization of critical incidents

After interviewing 10 people, you may obtain a list of approximately 200 critical incidents. This list will contain incidents that are similar to each other. These should be grouped together. The key to categorizing these critical incidents is to focus on a specific adjective or verb they share. After forming the clusters, write a phrase for each cluster which reflects the content of its incidents. This phrase is called a *satisfaction item*. One guideline in writing the satisfaction items is that they should contain a specific descriptive term of the service or product or a verb that describes an actual event involving the service or product. For example, the following three critical incidents, each from different people, would fall under one satisfaction item:

1. I waited too long before I was helped.
2. I was in a big hurry but had to wait in line for a very long time.
3. I waited in line for a very short time.

A satisfaction item which would encompass these three similar incidents could be:

I waited a short period of time before I was helped.

As indicated by this example, both positive and negative critical incidents can be included under one satisfaction item. The three critical incidents listed above, even though they reflect positive and negative aspects of service, are all reflected by the verb "wait." Therefore, the satisfaction item was written to include the word "wait."

Writing satisfaction items may take some practice. The most important thing to remember is that satisfaction items, like critical incidents, should be specific in describing the service or product. Quite often, the satisfaction item might even be one of the critical incidents.

Once all the critical incidents are categorized into their respective satisfaction items, repeat the categorization process using the satisfaction items. Now, group similar satisfaction items to form a specific customer requirement or quality dimension. Label these customer requirements with phrases or a single word describing the content of the satisfaction items. These summary labels reflect the specific quality dimensions. Unlike the satisfaction items, these labels do not have to be specific. The only requirement is that the label should reflect the content of the satisfaction items. Using the example above, we may generate a second satisfaction item which results in these two satisfaction items:

1. I waited a short period of time before I was helped.
2. Service started promptly when I arrived.

Both of these satisfaction items would be included under one customer requirement category labeled:

Responsiveness of service

Thus, after finishing all the groupings, you will obtain a hierarchical relationship representing three levels of specificity. The three levels fall on a specific–general continuum. The critical incidents fall on the specific end of the continuum; the satisfaction items fall somewhere in between the ends; and the customer requirements fall on the general end of the continuum.

Although the outlined process leads from critical incidents directly to satisfaction items which lead, in turn, to customer requirements, this is not the only order in which the critical incidents approach can flow. It may be easier to first categorize the critical incidents directly into the customer requirement categories. Next, within each customer requirement category, categorize critical incidents into various satisfaction items. Thus, both methods result in a hierarchical relationship between critical incidents, satisfaction items, and customer requirements. This hierarchical relationship is illustrated in Figure 2.1. Customer requirements are defined by satisfaction items which are, in turn, defined by critical incidents.

Three forms are presented in appendix A and B to help you conduct interviews to determine the critical incidents. These forms are designed to facilitate each step in the critical incidents approach. The first form (Appendix A) will help you divide positive and negative aspects of the service and will make it easier to list all the critical incidents in a simple format. After you have conducted all the interviews, you can cut out the critical incidents and allocate them into separate satisfaction items. The second form (Appendix B) will allow you to place critical incidents into clusters and write satisfaction items as headings for each cluster. After writing all the satisfaction items, you can place similar satisfaction items in one customer requirement category. The third form (Appendix B) allows you to list satisfaction items which fall under a particular customer requirement.

QUALITY OF THE CATEGORIZATION PROCESS

The allocation process (from incident to satisfaction item, and from satisfaction item to customer requirement category) is very critical in understanding quality dimensions. Since the resulting customer requirements are derived from the allocation process of critical incidents, it is important to determine the quality of this allocation process.

The quality of both steps of the grouping processes can be established by having two people involved in the allocation process. These people will be referred to as judges since their role involves judging the similarity of critical incidents and satisfaction items. The first judge will follow the process above, grouping the incidents into satisfaction items, and then grouping the satisfaction items into customer requirement categories. The second judge is given the customer requirement categories established by the first judge and asked to allocate the critical incidents directly into them, bypassing the satisfaction items.

Interjudge agreement

The quality of the allocation process is indicated by the extent of agreement between the two judges. This "interjudge agreement" is the percentage of incidents both judges place in the same customer requirement category. Interjudge agreement is calculated by dividing the number of same incidents both judges place in the same customer requirement category by the total number of redundant and distinct incidents both judges placed in the category. The index can range from 0 to 1.0. As this index approaches 1.0, it indicates that the judges are in high agreement. When the index approaches 0, it indicates that the judges are in low agreement. An index of approximately .8 should be used as a cutoff to determine if the customer requirement was acceptable. This criteria has been suggested elsewhere (Latham, et al., 1979).

Let's take an example to illustrate this index. Suppose the first judge grouped 100 critical incidents into 20 satisfaction items. Next, assume that this judge allocated two satisfaction items (a total of seven incidents) into one particular customer requirement category. Specifically, judge 1 included incidents 1, 4, 6, 7, 9, 13, and 40 into the customer requirement category of *availability*. Next, the second judge would allocate all 100 critical incidents directly into the customer requirement categories

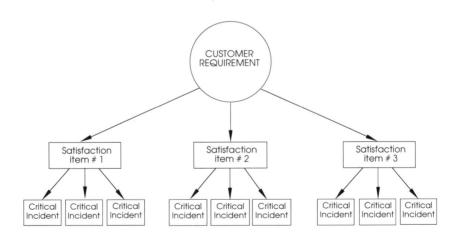

FIGURE 2.1 Hierarchical relationship among critical incidents, satisfaction items, and customer requirement

that were established by the first judge, skipping the allocation of incidents into satisfaction items. Suppose that judge 2 included incidents 1, 2, 4, 6, 7, 9, 13, and 40 into the *availability* customer requirement category. The interjudge agreement for this particular category would be .88 (7/8). The interjudge agreement index would also be calculated for the remaining customer requirement categories.

If the criteria of .8 is not obtained, one or both judges may have made an error in the categorization process. A judge may have accidentally included/omitted a critical incident because he/she did not read the incident or category correctly. Thus, a brief check of the critical incidents could correct this problem. Also, a low interjudge index could occur when a small number of incidents make up one customer requirement. Therefore, if one judge omitted one incident from a total possible set of four incidents, the resulting interjudge agreement would be .75 (3/4). Although this value is below the recommended cutoff of .8, it seems to be an acceptable value given the small number of incidents that comprise the customer requirement category.

If a low interjudge agreement index is apparent, both judges should discuss their disagreement and come to a consensus as to the appropriate incidents that compose a particular customer requirement category. If they cannot agree, a third judge could be included to categorize the incidents into the categories. This third judge could highlight the differences between the first two judges, which will lead to some consensus.

COMPREHENSIVENESS OF THE CUSTOMER REQUIREMENTS

Customer requirements obtained from the interviews should comprehensively define the quality of the service or product. If one important customer requirement category is overlooked during the initial interviewing process, the resulting customer satisfaction questionnaire would be deficient in measuring all customer requirements. In other words, you would be unable to assess your customers' perception on an important element of your service or product. Subsequently, you might not be able to improve overall customer satisfaction, because you do not know why your customers are satisfied or dissatisfied.

You may also establish the quality of the content of critical incidents (Latham, et al., 1979). Do this by removing a random group of approximately 10 percent of the critical incidents from the initial list *before* they are categorized into satisfaction items and customer requirement categories. After the entire allocation process is completed with 90 percent of the critical incidents (determining customer requirements category),

RESPONSIVENESS OF SERVICE

I.   I waited a short period of time before I was helped.
   1. I waited too long before I was helped.
   2. Lines were too long.
   3. I waited in line for a very long time.

II.   The service started immediately when I arrived.
   4. I went into the bank and the teller responded immediately to me.
   5. I received immediate service for my transaction.
   6. I could not get the teller's attention even though I was the only one in line.

SPEED OF TRANSACTION

III. The teller handled transactions in a short period of time.
   7. The teller handled transactions fast.
   8. The handling of the transaction was quick after I told him what I wanted.

IV.   The teller took a long time to complete my transaction.
   9. The entire transaction took too long.
   10. I waited a long time once I got to the window.

AVAILABILITY OF SERVICE

V.   The financial consultant was available to schedule me for an appointment at a good time.
   11. I was able to set up an appointment with a financial consultant at a good time.
   12. The appointment time with the financial planner was when I wanted it.

VI.   My appointment with the financial consultant was at a convenient time.
   13. The financial planner was available at a convenient time.
   14. My appointment was at an inconvenient time.

PROFESSIONALISM

VII. The teller talked to me in a pleasant way.
   15. The teller took the time to talk to me to get all my requests completed.
   16. The teller was rude to me (specifically, he was short with me).
   17. The teller yelled at me when I could not open the depository canister.

TABLE 2.4 Critical incidents, satisfaction items, and customer requirements related to the banking industry

VIII. The teller was very personable.
    18. The teller gave a personal compliment on my appearance.
    19. The teller had a friendly smile.
    20. The teller was not personal (did not say hello or goodbye).

IX. The teller carefully listened to me when I was requesting a transaction.
    21. The teller carefully listened to my request.
    22. The teller took the time to listen to me when I requested a lot of things.

X. The teller knew how to handle the transactions.
    23. The teller knew how to handle a special transaction I requested.
    24. The teller had to ask for help from another teller for a special transaction I asked for.
    25. The teller looked confused when I asked for a special transaction.

OVERALL SATISFACTION WITH SERVICE

XI. The quality of the way the teller treated me was high.

XII. The way the teller treated me met my expectations.

XIII. I am satisfied with the way the teller treated me.

TABLE 2.4 continued

examine the remaining 10 percent to see if they can be placed in the customer requirements categories.

If the 10 percent clearly can be placed into the customer requirement categories, then the categories are probably a comprehensive list of all possible customer requirement categories for that organization or group. If one or more of the 10 percent cannot be placed into any customer requirement categories, then the list is probably deficient in defining all possible customer requirement categories. This problem can be handled by interviewing more customers to obtain more critical incidents. The recommended number of additional interviews, however, will depend on the extent of the deficiency; the more deficient, the more interviews are needed. As a general rule, you should conduct five additional interviews for every critical incident that could not be allocated in the initial list of customer requirements. Once you have conducted these additional interviews, reallocate all critical incidents into satisfaction items, and then into customer requirement categories.

INTERIOR QUALITY

I.   The seating position was very comfortable.
    1. The seats are comfortable.
    2. The seats were very uncomfortable.
    3. There is ample leg room.

II.   The visibility through the window was good.
    4. There were many blind spots from the driver's seat.

III. The inside of the car was noisy.
    5. There is loud interior noise.
    6. The interior noise interfered with the sound of the stereo.
    7. Air whistles through the window.
    8. There was little noise while I was driving.

INSTRUMENTATION

IV.   The instrumentation panel was simple to understand.
    9. Instrumentation panel is difficult to read.
    10. The dials for the accessories were too complex to understand.
    11. The dials for the controls were easy to understand.

V.   The instrumentation panel was clearly visible from the driving seat.
    12. I could clearly see all the instruments and gauges.
    13. I had a clear view of the instrumentation.
    14. Instruments are within good reaching distance.

"DRIVABILITY"

VI.   The car stopped smoothly when I applied the brakes.
    15. The car did not brake well. (It would vibrate when I was braking.)
    16. The car vibrated when I applied the brakes.
    17. The car stopped smoothly when I applied the brakes.

VII. The car vibrated at high speeds.
    18. The car vibrated at high speeds.
    19. The car rides smooth, even at high speeds.

VIII. The car handled corners well.
    20. The car handles corners well.
    21. I could negotiate corners very well.
    22. The car would consistently skid around tight corners.

TABLE 2.5 Critical incidents, satisfaction items, and customer requirements related to the driving quality of automobiles

OVERALL SATISFACTION WITH AUTOMOBILE

IX.   I enjoyed driving the car.

X.   I liked the overall driving experience of the car.

XI.   The drive was excellent.

TABLE 2.5 continued

The next part of this chapter illustrates the use of the critical incidents technique to determine customer requirements in the service and manufacturing sectors. The service sector is represented by the banking industry, and the manufacturing sector is represented by the automobile industry. In addition, because customers can be internal to an organization, there is an illustration of the critical incidents approach as applied to a department which provides statistical support to other departments in the organization.

BANKING INDUSTRY

The first step in this process included interviews of 10 people who have had interactions with the bank's service. Critical incidents are confined to those related to customer interactions with personnel in the banking facility.

Critical incidents obtained from each person resulted in a total of 146 incidents. Some of these incidents appear in Table 2.4. In addition, the table includes the ten satisfaction items (preceded by Roman numerals) that represent their respective critical incidents. Furthermore, satisfaction items are grouped into four customer requirement categories.

There is also a category labeled *Overall Satisfaction with Service*. The satisfaction items for this category are less specific than the items in different customer requirement categories and are not based on any critical incidents. This category represents overall service quality; it is not focused on any particular quality dimension. The value of these items will become clear in Chapters 3 and 5.

It is important to note that customer requirements reflect only aspects of the banking industry that are related to financial personnel. Additional incidents could have been included from other aspects of the bank-

STATISTICAL SUPPORT

I.   The staff person explained the statistical tests in understandable words.
      1. There was good explanation on statistical tests.
      2. I received good explanation on statistical analyses.

II.   The statistical analyses were thorough.
      3. There was good analysis of data.
      4. Statistical help was minimal.
      5. The data analysis was incomplete.

III. The staff understood my software requirements.
      6. The software problem was never resolved.
      7. The staff understood the kinds of software I needed.

ENTHUSIASM

IV.   The staff person was always willing to help.
      8. The person was always willing to help.
      9. The person would always help when I asked.

V.   The staff person went out of his/her way to help.
      10. The person did not do the tasks.
      11. The person refused to do the project.
      12. The person did not do the project I asked them to do.

FINAL WRITTEN REPORT

VI.   The written report was sufficiently detailed.
      13. The writeup of the project was not detailed.
      14. The written report was not complete.
      15. The document needed to be more comprehensive.

VII. The written report contained what I needed.
      16. Everything I asked for was in the final report.
      17. The report contained everything I asked for.

RESPONSIVENESS

VIII. The staff person completed the job quickly.
      18. Projects are completed quickly.
      19. The project started very late.
      20. I received fast turn-around time on my project.

TABLE 2.6 Critical incidents, satisfaction items, and customer requirements related to the quality of a statistical support department

PROJECT MANAGEMENT

IX.   The staff person finished the project in the stated time frame.
      21. The staff person did not meet the specified deadlines.
      22. The staff person did not have the job completed for a meeting.
      23. The project was turned in late.

X.   The staff person planned the entire project through its completion.
      24. The planning of the project was complete.
      25. The project was well-organized.

XI.   The staff person understood how much time the project required.
      26. The person did not understand my requirements.
      27. The person understood the magnitude of the project.

OVERALL SATISFACTION WITH SUPPORT

XII. I am satisfied with the service I received.

XIII. The quality of the service met my expectations.

TABLE 2.6 continued

ing industry, such as phone transaction banking, automatic teller machines, and banking statements.

AUTOMOBILE INDUSTRY

The next illustration of the critical incidents technique applies to the automobile industry. Critical incidents were confined to the aspects of the automobile's interior and its "drivability." Aspects of car driving quality were gathered in customer interviews. The critical incidents, satisfaction items, and customer requirements appear in Table 2.5. The categorization process resulted in three customer requirements.

   Another way to conceptualize the groupings of these satisfaction items is to place them all into one customer requirement category called *perception of driving quality*. This customer requirement could be paralleled by another aspect of car quality such as *reliability of car*. This customer requirement might be measured by more objective indices such as the number of repairs, amount of money spent on repairs, or number of breakdowns. Therefore, using this conceptualization, there could be two

QUALITY DIMENSION DEVELOPMENT

Steps	Important Points
1. Create list of quality dimensions.	■ Read professional and trade journals to obtain list of quality dimensions. ■ Generate list from personal experience.
2. Write definitions of each dimension.	■ Definition can be in general terms.
3. Develop specific examples for each quality dimension.	■ Examples should use specific adjectives reflecting the service or product. ■ Examples should include specific behaviors of the provider. ■ Examples should use declarative statements.

CRITICAL INCIDENTS APPROACH

Steps	Important Points
1. Generate critical incidents.	■ Interview customers. ■ Critical incidents should be specific examples of good or poor service or product quality. ■ Each critical incident reflects only one example.
2. Categorize critical incidents into clusters.	■ Categorization is based on similarity in content of the incidents.

TABLE 2.7 Procedures for establishing customer requirements

Steps	Important Points
3. Write satisfaction items for each critical incident cluster.	▪ Each satisfaction item should be a declarative statement. ▪ Satisfaction items should be specific.
4. Categorize satisfaction items into clusters, each cluster representing a customer requirement.	▪ Categorization should be based on similarity of satisfaction items. ▪ Customer requirement must reflect the content of satisfaction items.
5. Determine the quality of the categorization process.	▪ Two judges should do categorization steps. ▪ Calculate interjudge agreement.
6. Determine the comprehensiveness of customer requirements.	▪ Remove 10% of the critical incidents before establishing customer requirements. ▪ Determine if the 10% can be placed into the customer requirements.

TABLE 2.7 continued

customer requirements: 1) the customers' perception of driving quality, and 2) the car's reliability.

STATISTICAL SUPPORT

The next illustration of the critical incidents technique applies to a statistical department that provides support to other departments within the organization. A total of nine customers who have had previous contact with the staff in this department were interviewed. The categorization process resulted in five customer requirements. A partial list of the critical incidents, satisfaction items, and customer requirements is included in Table 2.6.

SUMMARY

This chapter demonstrated two techniques for determining customer requirements, those aspects of your service or product that define its quality. The first technique, the quality dimension development process, involves people closely linked to the service or product. These people should be knowledgeable in understanding the needs of the customers and the function and purpose of the service or product. These people are responsible for determining quality dimensions, definitions of the quality dimensions, and specific examples of each dimension.

The second technique, the critical incident technique, involves obtaining information from customers about actual incidents they consider to define good and bad aspects of the product or service. These incidents define the satisfaction items, and the satisfaction items, in turn, define the customer requirements. Some examples demonstrated the effectiveness of the critical incidents approach in establishing customer requirements for both non-manufacturing and manufacturing organizations and internal customer support groups.

Table 2.7 presents the basic steps to follow for each method when establishing your customer requirements. This table includes some important points at each step to facilitate the process of establishing customer requirements.

The next chapter will discuss measurement issues related to questionnaire development and use. These measurement principles should be considered when evaluating any type of questionnaire designed to measure people's opinions, perceptions, and attitudes.

Three

ASSESSING YOUR CUSTOMERS' PERCEPTIONS AND ATTITUDES

Issues of Reliability and Validity

Measurement instruments can help us better understand and make predictions about our world. For example, we may be interested in measuring our customers' level of satisfaction to uncover any perceived problems with our service or product. In addition, we might want to change our customers' opinions about our service or product. To know our customers' current level of satisfaction and to realize if changes in their opinion do occur, we need a measure that accurately assesses customer attitudes. When we develop questionnaires, it is important to ensure that the data obtained from them reflect reliable and valid information. This chapter presents measurement issues that demonstrate the importance of careful thought when designing questionnaires to measure perceptions and attitudes.

THE MEANING OF CUSTOMER PERCEPTION AND ATTITUDE

Customers' perceptions of the quality of a service and their overall satisfaction have some observable indicators. Customers may smile when they talk about the product or service. They may say good things about the product or service. Both these actions are manifestations or indicators of an underlying construct we might call "customer satisfaction." The terms "customer satisfaction" and "perception of quality" are labels we use to summarize a set of observable actions related to the product

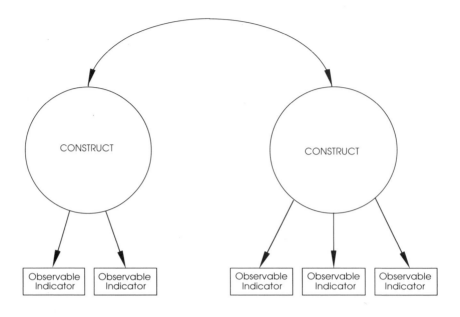

FIGURE 3.1 The relationship between observable indicators and the underlying constructs and the relationship between the constructs

and/or service. This idea of constructs and their relationship to observable variables is depicted in Figure 3.1.

As indicated by Figure 3.1, various observable criteria (e.g., items) might be manifestations of an underlying dimension (e.g., customer requirements). For example, we could make inferences about people's happiness by obtaining several types of observable indicators of the underlying *happiness* construct. Observable indicators could include smiling, laughing, and saying positive things. If a person is laughing, smiling, and saying positive things, we draw the conclusion that this person is happy. We have, in fact, concluded that this person is happy by examining the observable criteria.

Similarly, we draw conclusions about customers' perceptions and attitudes about products or services by examining observable manifestations related to the product or service. These observable manifestations are the responses the customers give on a customer satisfaction questionnaire. If people indicate good things about the product on the customer satisfaction questionnaire, and demonstrate other indications of positive behavior, we can draw the conclusion that they are satisfied with the product.

From Figure 3.1, we can make some conclusions about the concept of customer perception and attitude. First, we can never really know the true underlying satisfaction level of our customers. We develop measures to make *inferences* about the underlying construct, satisfaction. Second, we are interested in the relationship between underlying dimensions or constructs (e.g., *customer satisfaction* or *perceived responsiveness*). We want to understand how these underlying constructs, or customer requirements, are related to each other.

When constructing a questionnaire or scale that assesses customer attitudes and perceptions toward customer requirements, it is necessary to consider measurement issues to ensure that scores derived from such instruments reflect accurate information about these underlying constructs. The emphasis on measurement issues in customer satisfaction is similar to the importance of measurement issues concerning instruments designed to measure tangible objects, such as parts of a machine. Gauge repeatability and reliability (Gauge R&R) indices, for example, are designed to reflect the quality of the measurement process in industrial settings. Similarly, statistical indices can reflect the quality of measurement of satisfaction questionnaires. Two important measurement issues to consider when developing questionnaires are *reliability* and *validity*.

RELIABILITY

I will introduce the concept of reliability using a simple measurement example. We could use a ruler to measure the length of one particular part. We could measure the part five times, obtaining five scores. Even though the part can be characterized by one true length, we would expect the five scores to be slightly different from each other. The deviation could be due to various random factors in the measurement process, such as variations in use of the ruler with each measurement, or change in ruler length with each measurement. To the extent that random factors are introduced into the measurement process, any one score we obtain may not reliably reflect the true score.

When we develop a questionnaire that assesses customers' perception of the quality of the service or product, we want to be sure that measurements are free from random error. That is, we want to be sure the true underlying level of perception of quality or satisfaction is accurately reflected in the questionnaire score. When random error is introduced into measurement, the observed score is less reliable in estimating the true underlying score. Errors of measurement are examined under the context of reliability.

Reliability is defined as the extent to which measurements are free from random-error variance. Random error decreases the reliability of the measurement. If we want to feel confident that scores on our questionnaire reliably reflect the underlying dimension, we want the questionnaire to demonstrate high reliability. There are three general forms of reliability: test–retest reliability, equivalent form reliability, and internal consistency. This discussion will focus on internal consistency. Discussions of the other forms of reliability appear in various textbooks (Anastasi, 1988; Brown, 1983; Guion, 1965; and Gulliksen, 1987). I will first review information concerning classical measurement theory, and then I will discuss indices used to estimate the reliability of questionnaires. A more detailed discussion of classical measurement theory, including underlying statistical assumptions, appears in various books (e.g., Gulliksen, 1987).

Classical measurement theory

When assessing a customer's level of satisfaction, the best we can do is to ask the person to respond to some questions. From the answers, we obtain a score which indicates that person's level of satisfaction with the product or service. However, this only gives us an observed score of that person's level of satisfaction. According to classical measurement theory, this observed score is composed of a true score (which is the actual level of satisfaction) and a component of measurement error. Error is assumed to be random and is unrelated to the true score. The basic equation of classical measurement theory, known as the classical measurement model, describes the relationship between observed scores, true scores, and error. The model is:

$$X = T + E$$

where X is the observed score, T is the true score, and E is error of measurement. To the extent that we have small error of measurement, this observable measure (X) is highly representative of the underlying true score, T.

An illustration concerning the relationship between these three components might make things clear. In Table 3.1, we have a hypothetical example of some data collected from 10 customers. The first column (X) represents the score these people received on the questionnaire (their observed score) and indicates their level of satisfaction: the higher the number, the higher their satisfaction. Now, let's assume that we were somehow able to obtain the customers' true level of satisfaction (the customers' true score)—perhaps we know God, and He informed us of the true level of satisfaction for each customer. The second column (T) represents the customers' true level of satisfaction. Finally, the last column (E) represents the random error and is calculated by subtracting the values in column T from the values in column X.

There are two approaches we can take in explaining reliability. One approach focuses on correlational analysis (see Appendix J), and the other focuses on variance for each of the components in the classical theory equation (X, T, and E). I will present the correlational approach first.

Using correlational analysis, we can determine the degree of agreement between the observed scores (X) and the true scores (T). We can calculate the correlation coefficient between X and T scores. A correlation coefficient can range from –1 to 1. A negative correlation indicates that as one variable increases, the other variable decreases. A positive correlation indicates that as one variable increases, the other variable also increases. A correlation of zero indicates there is no linear relationship between the two variables. A perfect negative or positive correlation indicates a perfect negative and positive relationship, respectively.

Using the data in Table 3.1, the correlation coefficient between the X and T scores is calculated to be .88. This suggests that the differences in true scores is closely matched by differences in observed scores. That is, people who have truly high scores (true scores) also obtain relatively high scores on the questionnaire (observed score). Also, people who have

Customers	X	T	E	
1.	5	5	0	Average for:
2.	3	4	–1	$X = M_X = \Sigma X_i / n$
3.	4	3	1	$T = M_T = \Sigma T_i / n$
4.	3	2	1	$E = M_E = \Sigma E_i / n$
5.	1	1	0	
6.	5	5	0	
7.	5	4	1	Variance for:
8.	2	3	–1	$X = \text{Var}(X) = \Sigma(X_i - M_X)^2 / n$
9.	1	2	–1	$T = \text{Var}(T) = \Sigma(T_i - M_T)^2 / n$
10.	1	1	0	$E = \text{Var}(E) = \Sigma(E_i - M_E)^2 / n$

$$M_X = 3.0 \quad M_T = 3.0 \quad M_E = 0.0$$
$$\text{Var}(X) = 2.88 \quad \text{Var}(T) = 2.22 \quad \text{Var}(E) = .66$$

TABLE 3.1 Hypothetical example illustrating observed scores, true scores, and error

relatively low true scores also obtain relatively low observed scores on the questionnaire.

Therefore, a form of reliability would be the correlation between observed and true scores. As the correlation between X and T increases, the differences in people's X scores more closely approximates the differences in people's T scores. When the correlation between X and T is 1.00, there is perfect linear agreement between X and T; that is, differences in X scores exactly match the differences in T scores. When the correlation between X and T is 0, there is no linear relationship between X and T; that is, there is no agreement between X and T scores.

We could also examine reliability of the measurement instrument by focusing on variance of the specific components (i.e., observed, true, and error components). Variance is an index which reflects the spread of the data around the arithmetic average of the data. (See Appendix E for a discussion of average and variance.) The larger the variance, the larger the spread of the data around the average. The formula for variance is presented in Table 3.1, and the variance for each component has been calculated. The variances for each of the sets of variables are related in a similar fashion as the variables themselves:

$$\text{Var}(X) = \text{Var}(T) + \text{Var}(E)$$

where $\text{Var}(X)$ is the variance associated with the set of observed scores, $\text{Var}(T)$ is the variance associated with the set of true scores, and $\text{Var}(E)$ is the variance associated with the set of errors.

As error variance decreases, as is indicated by the equation, the variance of the observed score approaches the variance of the true score; that is, as error decreases, the differences in observed scores between people become a *reliable* reflection of differences in their true scores. If the error variance is large, however, the observed score is not reliably related to the true score.

Reliability estimates can be indexed by a number which represents the percentage of variance of observed scores that is accounted for by the variance in true scores. In mathematical terms, this corresponds to the following equation:

$$\text{Reliability } (r_{xx'}) = \text{Var}(T) / (\text{Var}(T) + \text{Var}(E))$$
$$\text{where } \text{Var}(T) + \text{Var}(E) = \text{Var}(X).$$

This reliability index can range from 0 to 1.0. A reliability index of 1.0 indicates there is no measurement error; observed scores can be perfectly predicted by true scores. This is a highly desirable situation. A reliability index of 0 indicates there is no true score variation, or that the variation in the observed scores can be completely explained by random error.

This is a highly undesirable situation. For the data in Table 3.1, we can calculate the reliability of the observed score (X), which is $r_{xx'} = 2.22/2.88 = .77$. This indicates that our observed scores are somewhat related to the underlying true scores for the customers. In fact, the correlation between the X and T scores can be calculated by taking the square root of the reliability ($r_{XT} = \sqrt{.77} = .88$). Conversely, reliability is the squared correlation between the observed scores and true scores.

Reliability, then, can be discussed in terms of both the relationship between observed and true scores, and the variance of components of the classical measurement model. The two approaches should not be interpreted as representing two different types of reliability. They are merely two different ways of conceptualizing the degree to which observed scores are related to true scores (or the degree to which observed scores are free from random error). The reader is offered both approaches to help facilitate understanding of this important concept.

Standard error of measurement

Measurement error is often discussed in terms of the standard error of measurement (SEM). The SEM could be calculated for a given individual by administering the questionnaire or test to that individual many times (say, 100 times). Due to measurement error, the person might not get the same score on each administration of the test. Thus, these observed scores would form a distribution which would approximate a normal distribution described by a mean and a standard deviation (see Appendix F). The mean of this distribution would be our *best estimate* of the person's true score. The standard deviation of this distribution is technically called the standard error of measurement and describes the amount of measurement error we have. Theoretically, we could calculate the SEM for each individual, but this would be tedious, if not impossible. We can more easily calculate SEM from the reliability of the questionnaire. The equation for the SEM is presented below:

$$SEM = s_x * \sqrt{(1 - r_{xx'})}$$

where s_x is the standard deviation of observed scores for the sample of people to which the questionnaire was administered, and $r_{xx'}$ is the reliability of the questionnaire.

As this formula illustrates, SEM is inversely and monotonically related to reliability. That is, for a given s_x, an increase in reliability always leads to a decrease in SEM. As reliability approaches 1.0 (observed scores, X, are perfectly correlated with true scores, T), SEM goes to zero. Con-

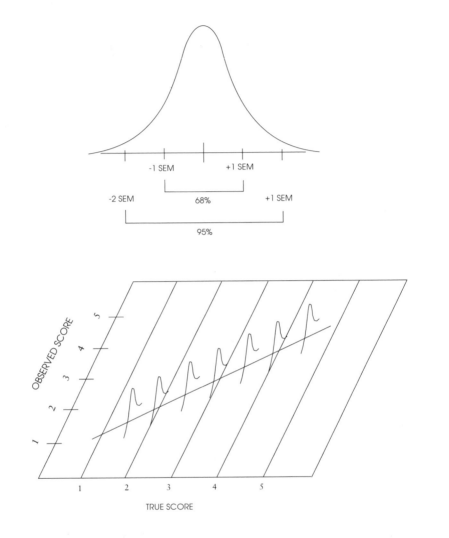

FIGURE 3.2 The top portion illustrates an expected distribution of observed scores for a given person. The bottom portion illustrates the relationship between observed scores and true scores and incorporates the standard error of measurement.

versely, as reliability approaches zero (X scores are not related to T scores), SEM will equal the s_x.

The meaning of SEM and the relationship between reliability and SEM is illustrated in Figure 3.2. The top portion of the figure presents the expected distribution of random errors for a given individual using a particular questionnaire. The SEM describes the degree of errors for observed scores we would expect for a given true score. As the SEM decreases, the more confident we are that the observed scores are a good reflection of the true scores. For example, if the SEM for a given questionnaire was .50, then we could say with a 95 percent degree of confidence that, for a person with a true score of 4, his/her observed score would fall between 3.0 = (4 − (2*.5)) and 5.0 = (4 + (2*.5)). If the SEM was .25, we could say with the same degree of confidence that the person's observed score falls between 3.5 and 4.5.

The bottom portion of this figure demonstrates the relationship between X and T scores and shows how SEM is incorporated into this relationship. As this illustration indicates, if we have a high degree of measurement error, we are less confident that a particular observed score is associated with any one true score. For example, if SEM is high, which would be reflected in the widening of the distributions, then an observed score of 4 might represent a true score of 4 or it might also represent a number of other true scores. If SEM is low, which would be reflected in the narrowing of the distributions, then an observed score of 3 would most likely represent a true score of 3, and the possibility of the observed score representing other true scores is greatly decreased.

Some simple scatter plots of the relationship between the X and T scores are presented in Figure 3.3. Although T scores can never be assessed, a *hypothetical* scatterplot of the T scores with the X scores can be presented given a certain value of the reliability. In general, as reliability increases, the precision in predicting X scores from the T scores increases. In other words, as reliability increases, the variability in X for any given T score (represented as SEM) decreases. As seen in Figure 3.3(a), a reliability of 0 indicates that changes in X scores are unrelated to changes in T scores. In other words, a given observed score, X, could reflect many possible true scores, T. As seen in Figure 3.3(b), a reliability of .81 indicates that an observed score (X) is highly related to the underlying true score (T). Consequently, a given observed score is likely to reflect a limited number of true scores. Figure 3.3(c) illustrates a measure with a low degree of reliability.

RELIABILITY ESTIMATES

Conceptually, reliability reflects how well the observed scores are related to the true scores. Unlike our hypothetical example in which God informed us of the true level of customers' satisfaction, we do not know their true level of satisfaction. Because we do not know the true scores, we are unable to directly calculate the correlation between the observed

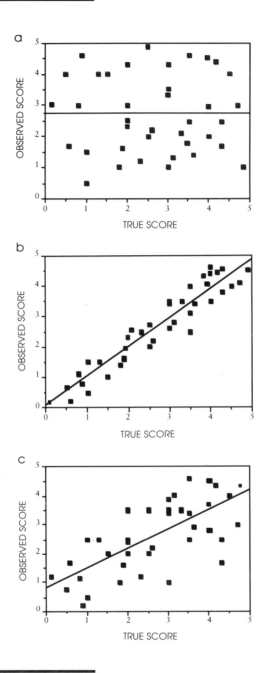

FIGURE 3.3 The hypothetical relationship between true scores and observed scores with varying degrees of reliability (a: $r_{xx'} = 0$; b: $r_{xx'} = .81$; c: $r_{xx'} = .25$)

scores and true scores, and are thus unable to calculate the reliability with the equation presented above. There are various formulae, however, to estimate the reliability of questionnaires. Two of these estimates will be presented here. They are split-half reliability and Cronbach's alpha (Cronbach, 1951). These estimates are called internal consistency estimates, and generally tell you how well the items in the scale are interrelated. The higher the interrelationship between the items, the higher the reliability of the overall scale.

Split-half reliability estimate

This method estimates internal consistency by dividing the scale into halves (e.g., odd vs. even items, or first half of scale vs. last half of scale), then correlating the scores on these halves. A high correlation indicates that the two sets yield consistent information; that is, if a person scores high on one set of items, then that person also scores high on the other set. Thus, the items are likely measuring the same thing.

When using the split-half method to estimate reliability, it is necessary to include a correction factor. Reliability estimates are affected by the length of the scale: the more items on the scale, the higher the reliability. Using the split-half method, we actually estimate the reliability for a scale that was half the original length (because the scale was divided in half). To control for test length, we use a correction formula, the Spearman-Brown formula, which results in a corrected reliability estimate. The general formula is:

$r_{cc'} = (nr_{12}) / (1 + (n - 1)r_{12})$; where $r_{cc'}$ is the corrected reliability estimate of the questionnaire, r_{12} is the correlation between the two halves of the same questionnaire, and n is the number of items in the overall scale divided by the number of items in each of the halves

For example, we may want to calculate the reliability of a questionnaire that has 10 items. Using the split-half method, we divide the questionnaire into halves containing five items each and calculate the correlation between the halves. Suppose we found that the correlation was $r_{12} = .7$. Next, because reliability estimates are affected by the length of the scale, we would correct this value to obtain a better estimate of reliability. The final reliability estimate, corrected for length, would be $r_{cc'} = .82$ $(r_{cc'} = (2*.7)/(1 + .7))$.

Cronbach's alpha estimate

The Cronbach's alpha estimate also tells us how highly the items in our questionnaire are interrelated. Unlike the split-half reliability method,

	Avail1	Avail2	Avail3	Resp1	Resp2	Resp3
Avail1	1.00	.92	.80	.23	.00	.34
Avail2	.92	1.00	.51	.49	.16	.49
Avail3	.80	.51	1.00	-.25	-.25	.00
Resp1	.23	.49	-.25	1.00	.78	.83
Resp2	.00	.16	-.25	.78	1.00	.67
Resp3	.34	.49	.00	.83	.67	1.00

FIGURE 3.4 The correlation matrix of the items from Figure 4.2

however, this estimate does not have to be corrected for length. Calculation of Cronbach's estimate is usually done with the help of a statistical package designed to calculate this reliability estimate. Statistical packages are usually used if questionnaires have many items. Cronbach's (1951) estimate of reliability is calculated using the variance of individual items and covariances between the items. This estimate, however, also can be calculated using the correlations between the items. Given that items within a questionnaire use the same scale, both approaches give similar estimates. The latter approach is easier to understand and is presented here. Generally, the formula for Cronbach's reliability estimate is:

$$r_{xx'} = (K/(K-1)) * (1 - [(\Sigma X_{ii}) / (\Sigma X_{ii} + \Sigma X_{ij} \text{ where } i \neq j)])$$

where X_{iis} and X_{ijs} are the elements in the covariance matrix or correlation matrix, and K is the number of items within a given dimension. The numerator, (ΣX_{ii}), indicates that the elements in the diagonal of the covariance (correlation) matrix be added together. The denominator, $(\Sigma X_{ii} + \Sigma X_{ij})$, indicates that all the elements in the covariance (correlation) matrix be added together.

Figure 3.4 represents a correlation matrix using actual data for the items from Figure 4.2 in chapter 4 (page 58). Customers responded to each item using a five-point scale ("1" represented strong disagreement, and "5" represented strong agreement). With this questionnaire, we think we are measuring two customer requirements, perception of *availability* (items 1 through 3) and perception of *responsiveness* (items 4 through 6). Therefore, we can combine the items in their respective scales (average of the items within each scale) to obtain two observed scores, each representing a customer requirement. We now want to see if these observed scores are reliable indicators of an underlying dimension. The reliability estimate is .897 = (1.5* (1 – 3/7.468)) for perception of *availability* and .904 = (1.5* (1 – 3/7.556)) for perception of *respon-*

siveness. As indicated by these reliability estimates, the composite of the three items for each dimension gives us an overall observed score that is a reliable measure of the underlying dimension.

BENEFITS OF SCALES WITH HIGH RELIABILITY

There are two benefits of having a scale with high reliability: 1) it distinguishes between varying levels of satisfaction better than a scale with low reliability; and 2) it makes it more likely that we will find significant relationships between variables that are truly related to each other.

Detection of differences in satisfaction levels

Reliability indicates the degree to which observed scores are related to true scores. Therefore, if we use a scale with a high level of reliability, we can better distinguish between people on the continuum of customer satisfaction. As illustrated in the scatter plot in Figure 3.3(c) representing a scale of low reliability ($r_{xx'} = .25$), we would have considerable error of measurement. Consequently, we could find that customer 1, who has a true score of 3, could have an observed score between 1.0 and 4.5. Also, customer 2, who has a true score of 5.0, could have an observed score as low as 3.0. Although these two customers actually differ with respect to customer satisfaction (T scores), we might not be able to distinguish between them because our scale is unreliable. It is possible that customer 2 with a higher true score of customer satisfaction might get an observed score that is lower than the observed score of customer 1. With low reliability, there is a great deal of uncertainty as to what the observed score indicates for any person. This would limit the strength of the conclusions we can make about people's scores.

If we use a scale with high reliability such as $r_{xx'} = .81$ (see Figure 3.3(b)), we would have little error in measurement. Therefore, we would be able to distinguish between people whose satisfaction levels are close. Now, customer 1, who is truly less satisfied than customer 2, will more likely get an observed score that is lower than the score of customer 2. In the situation where reliability equals 1.0, customers who have a true score of 3 will get an observed score of 3, and customers who have a true score of 5 will get an observed score of 5.

In summary, when using scales with low reliability, only true differences that are very large are likely to be detected. A scale with high reliability will likely detect true differences that are either very large or very small. The strength of this detection is directly related to the reliability of the scale. Therefore, to increase the ability to make distinctions between customers, we need to increase the reliability of the scale.

Detection of significant relationships between variables

We might want to determine if perceptions of *availability* are linked to *overall customer satisfaction*. This might be important to know if we wanted to determine where to allocate some resources to increase overall customer satisfaction. We would allocate resources to increase *availability* of the service if, in fact, it did significantly predict *overall customer satisfaction*. We could determine how strongly these two variables are related to each other by calculating the correlation coefficient (see Appendix J) between them.

Even though we have an observed correlation between these two variables, we are really interested in the true correlation between them. Our observed scores possess some amount of measurement error which will decrease the correlation between these two variables. Due to error in measurement of the variables, observed correlations between variables are always smaller than the true correlations. The relationship between the true correlation and the observed correlation is:

$$r_{X_o Y_o} = r_{X_t Y_t} \sqrt{r_{XX'}} \sqrt{r_{YY'}}$$

where $r_{X_o Y_o}$ is the observed correlation between variables X and Y, $r_{X_t Y_t}$ is the true correlation between variables X and Y, and $\sqrt{r_{XX'}}$ and $\sqrt{r_{YY'}}$ are the reliabilities for variables X and Y respectively.

From this equation, we see that the observed correlation decreases as the reliability of either or both scales decreases. Also, as the reliability of both scales approaches unity, the observed correlation approaches the true correlation. Using the example above, even though there might be a true relationship between *availability* and *overall customer satisfaction*, poor measures (low reliability) of either variable would attenuate the correlation and lead us to the wrong conclusion about the relationship between these two variables.

For example, let's suppose that we assessed the satisfaction level of 50 of our customers using a measure that included scales assessing perception of *availability* and *overall customer satisfaction*. The reliability of each of these scales is .50. Suppose that the true correlation between these two variables is $r = .40$. With our sample of 50 customers, however, we might find an observed correlation of $r = .20 = (.40 * .71 * .71)$. Calculating the significance of this observed correlation coefficient, we find that it is not statistically significant from zero, $t(48) = 1.41, p >$ .05 (see Appendix J for explanation of t-tests for correlation coefficients). Thus, we incorrectly conclude that there is no relationship between these two variables even though a true relationship exists. With this misleading information, we may not allocate the necessary resources to *availability* and would miss an excellent opportunity to increase the satisfaction level of the customers.

An acceptable level of reliability will depend on how the questionnaire is used (see Nunnally, 1978). For basic research, as illustrated in the preceding paragraph, reliabilities should be .80 or higher. It has been stated, however, that increasing reliabilities above .80 will not dramatically affect the correlation between scales (Nunnally, 1978).

In summary, reliability of the scales will necessarily influence the magnitude of the correlation found between any two scales. The correlation is attenuated as the reliability of the scales decreases. Incorrect conclusions about the relationship between two variables are likely when the reliability of either or both scales is low.

FACTORS AFFECTING RELIABILITY

Various factors affect the reliability of scales. Two of them are the number of items in the scale, and the sample of people on which the reliability estimate is calculated.

Number of items in the scale

We can increase reliability by increasing the number of items in the scale. This is similar to the concept of decreasing sampling error by increasing sample size (see Appendix F). The more observations we have in our sample, the more confident we are that the sample mean is an accurate reflection of the population mean. Similarly, the more items we have in our questionnaire, the more confident we are that people's observed scores are accurate reflections of their true scores.

If increased reliability is to be realized by adding more items to the scale, the additional items must be representative of the same concept that is being measured. For example, if we have two dimensions in our questionnaire, *professionalism* and *responsiveness*, we could increase the reliability of the *responsiveness* scale by adding more items related to the responsiveness concept. These items, however, would not necessarily increase the reliability of the *professionalism* scale because they do not reflect that concept.

Sample of people

A sample of people who are similar with respect to their level of satisfaction might yield low reliability estimates of the scales. If a scale has potential scores ranging from 1 to 5, and everybody in the sample has a true score of 5, then, theoretically, there is no true score variance in this sample. Recall that reliability is the true score variance divided by the observed score variance. Therefore, in our example, if the true score variance is 0, then reliability would be calculated to be 0.

If we are to obtain high reliability estimates, we must base reliability estimates on a sample of people who are heterogeneous (they differ amongst themselves) with respect to the concept being measured. If people truly differ with respect to the concept being measured (true scores varying from 1 to 5), there would be true score variance in the sample. Consequently, because there will be considerable true score variance, we would more likely find a high reliability estimate.

THE NEED FOR MULTIPLE ITEMS IN MEASUREMENT

It must be noted that internal consistency indices can only be estimated with measures that have more than one item. In Table K.1 (page 152), the first three statements pertain to the dimension of *availability*. The next three statements pertain to *responsiveness*. A reader may ask, "Why use all these statements in the same customer satisfaction questionnaire? They seem to be redundant." The point of using multiple items to measure a given dimension is to ensure that our overall score, which is a composite of several observed scores, is a reliable reflection of the underlying true score. Measures that use only one item to assess a person's perception of quality of customer requirement categories or of overall customer satisfaction may be unreliable (not measuring the underlying true score). In fact, the reliability estimates presented above cannot be calculated for a one-item scale. Therefore, people who use one-item scales to assess the level of satisfaction of various customer requirements run the risk of obtaining information that is not highly reliable; that is, the observed score on their one-item measure is not highly related to the actual levels of satisfaction of their customers.

I think an illustration of the importance of multiple-item scales is warranted. Suppose that you wanted to develop one test to assess both simple arithmetic ability and reading comprehension. One way to assess arithmetic ability is to ask people to solve a mathematical problem, and one way to assess reading comprehension is to have people read a passage and then answer a question related to it. Does it seem reasonable to assess the level of mathematical ability by using a test that contains only one arithmetic question and to assess reading comprehension by using a test that contains only one problem? People who believe that one item reliably assesses the perception of customer requirements may also believe that one question is sufficient in measuring both the level of mathematical ability and the level of reading comprehension.

Mathematical ability and reading comprehension, like customer perceptions, are unobservable constructs measured by instruments (tests) that result in scores of some kind. According to classical measurement theory, these scores are only observable indications of the underlying level of satisfaction or level of mathematical or reading comprehension.

Intuitively we understand that to get a better indication of arithmetic ability and reading comprehension, we should use more than one question (item) to assess each ability. The more items related to a particular ability, the more confident we feel that the overall scores on that test will be consistently related to people's arithmetic ability and reading comprehension. In other words, we should have a test that has multiple items for each category we are measuring. In fact, with a test that contains multiple items for both arithmetic ability and reading comprehension, the reliability of each subscale can be calculated using the split-half method of estimating reliability. With this test, we would obtain two reliability estimates, one for the arithmetic scale and one for the reading comprehension scale.

The same argument for the importance of multiple items applies to measurement of customers' perceptions and attitudes. We should not feel comfortable with people who design customer satisfaction questionnaires to assess five quality dimensions using one item for each dimension. More than one item should be used when assessing customers' attitudes if we went to determine how reliably each dimension is measured.

Summary

So far, I have discussed issues of reliability or the internal consistency of measures. Internal consistency is concerned with how highly the scale items are interrelated with each other. When we are measuring customer perceptions or attitudes, we want items for that particular scale to be highly interrelated. This will lead to high reliability of the scale and will give us some confidence that observed scores derived from that measure reflect true levels of customer attitudes. Furthermore, we will be confident that the highly reliable measure will be able to distinguish between people who have a positive attitude and those who have a negative attitude.

Although reliability of a scale is crucial, it is not sufficient in determining the quality of a measure. We should also concern ourselves with the issue of validity.

VALIDITY

Validity refers to the degree to which evidence supports the *inferences* made from scores derived from measures, or the degree to which the scale measures what it is designed to measure. For example, if we make the inference that scores on a measure reflect levels of customer satisfaction, we need information to assess how well that inference is supported. Although we may have a highly reliable questionnaire, we still may want to question what the observed score actually indicates. Although the scale may reliably distinguish people on some underlying continuum, we still must ensure that the continuum is the correct continuum (e.g., customer satisfaction). Unlike mathematical indices of reliability, there is no one statistic that provides an overall index of the validity of inferences about scores. There are several ways to obtain evidence to support the inferences made from test scores. These methods, referred to as validity-related strategies (AERA, APA, & NCME, 1985), are: content-related strategy, criterion-related strategy, and construct-related strategy.

Content-related strategy

Content-related strategy is concerned with examining the content of the items of the scale. Content-related evidence is concerned with the degree to which items on the scale are representative of some "defined universe" or "domain of content."

Let's look at the assessment of customer satisfaction to demonstrate what kind of evidence should be examined. The domain or universe of content refers to all possible items that could be included in the customer satisfaction questionnaire. If we define our universe of content as those items which reflect satisfaction with the service provided, the questionnaire developed should have items representative of this defined universe. The goal of content validity is to have a set of items that best represents the universe; these items will compose our final questionnaire.

Examples of items appropriate for assessing customer satisfaction with service are "I am not happy with the way I was treated" or "The service was pleasant." These items are representative of what people would say if they were either dissatisfied or satisfied with the service they received. On the other hand, items that seem inappropriate for assessing customer satisfaction with service are "I am happy with the product" or "I am happy with the price I paid." These seem to be related to customers' attitudes toward the product received and the price of the service or product, rather than customer satisfaction with the service.

Content-related evidence involves the judgment of people familiar with the purpose of the questionnaire. These people determine the correspondence between the content domain and the items of the measure. The critical incidents approach outlined in chapter 2 is designed to ensure that the defined universe of important customer requirements is represented by the items in the customer satisfaction questionnaire.

Criterion-related strategy

Criterion-related strategy is concerned with examining the systematic relationship (usually in the form of a correlation coefficient) between scores on a given scale and other scores it should predict.

Again, I will use the customer satisfaction example to help illustrate a criterion-related strategy. You might be interested in how well the perception of various dimensions of quality predicts the extent to which people endorse the particular service (e.g., telling friends about it). These two constructs are conceptually different. The former focuses on customers' perceptions of the product's quality characteristics. The latter focuses on a particular behavior that may be predicted by people's level of satisfaction. The correlation between the measures of perceptions of quality and endorsement behavior represents a systematic relationship between these two variables. We would expect to find some dimensions of quality (as perceived by the customer) to be related to endorsement behavior with that product. The higher the quality, the more frequent the endorsements.

Construct-related strategy

In the field of psychology, a construct can be defined as an attribute or characteristic inferred from research (Guion, 1965). Construct-related evidence is derived from both previous validity strategies (content and criterion) and focuses on examining relationships between many variables. It is desirable to demonstrate two things when examining the correlations between measures. The first is that the scale correlates with variables with which it should correlate. This is termed *convergent validity*. The second is that the scale does not correlate with things with which it should not correlate. This is termed *discriminant validity* (Campbell and Fiske, 1959). We can establish evidence of convergent and discriminant validity by correlating test scores designed to measure the same thing and correlating test scores designed to measure different things, respectively.

Another approach in obtaining construct-related evidence is through the use of a multitrait-multimethod (MTMM) matrix (Campbell and Fiske, 1959). The MTMM approach requires the measurement of multiple constructs (or traits) through multiple measurement devices (or methods). The MTMM matrix is the correlation matrix of these constructs measured by different methods. The MTMM approach helps us determine the extent to which the correlations between constructs are due to the constructs (traits) being measured vs. the methods being used to measure them. Various patterns of correlations in the MTMM matrix indicate the extent to which the underlying constructs are being measured. We want to see high correlations between the measures of the same construct using different measurement instruments (evidence of convergent validity). We also want to see relatively low correlations— lower than the convergent validities—between the measures of different constructs using the same measurement instrument (evidence of discriminant validity).

Construct-related evidence also can be provided by examining the correlation between a given variable and other variables. The variable of interest is embedded in a theoretical framework. This framework can be theoretically derived and helps to define the meaning of the constructs being measured. This framework can tell us that this variable should correlate with certain variables and not with others. Using our previous example in discussing criterion-related strategies, the constructs *perception of quality* and *customer satisfaction* should be embedded into the theoretical framework of customer satisfaction. We would expect a measure of perceived quality to be related to a measure of customer satisfaction if we believe that the perceived quality of a product leads to customer satisfaction. However, we would not expect a relationship between customer satisfaction and, say, shoe size, since there is no theoretical reason why these two should be related. If we did find a relationship between these two variables, it could suggest that our measure of customer satisfaction is actually a poor measure. (It is possible, however, that the theoretical framework of customer satisfaction should be changed to include shoe size.)

Summary

Validity refers to the extent to which inferences from scores are meaningful. There are three methods of providing evidence for validity of scores on a customer satisfaction questionnaire. A content-related strategy focuses on the sample of items on the questionnaire and how well they represent the entire domain of customer satisfaction items. A criterion-related strategy focuses on statistical relationships between measures and whether scores predict what they should predict. A construct-related strategy is composed of the two former strategies and is more of a theory-driven method. It specifies to what the measure should and should not relate.

SUMMARY

This chapter discussed measurement issues of reliability and validity. Reliability refers to the degree to which observed scores obtained from a questionnaire are systematically related to some underlying true scores (i.e., the degree to which observed scores are free from random error). Reliability of scales is especially important when studying the relationship between variables. Low reliability decreases the observed correlation between two variables. Thus, if reliability of either or both measures is low, incorrect conclusions about the relationship between the variables are likely. Two formulae (split-half and Cronbach's alpha) help determine the reliability of summary scores. Although reliability is an important characteristic of a questionnaire, we must also concern ourselves with the *meaning* of the scores. We must ensure that the observed score represents the dimension we intend to measure. Validity refers to the degree to which we can make these types of inferences.

Four

CUSTOMER SATISFACTION QUESTIONNAIRE CONSTRUCTION

Item Generation, Response Format, and Item Selection

This chapter will give you some practical guidelines to follow when developing customer satisfaction questionnaires. In addition to reiterating the significance of customer requirements and satisfaction items, I will include new information on characteristics of good items, scaling procedures, and item selection. Finally, I will present a process for questionnaire construction integrating this information.

Customer satisfaction questionnaires are constructed in four phases: 1) determining questions (items) to be used in the questionnaire; 2) selecting the response format; 3) writing the introduction to the questionnaire; and 4) determining the content of the final questionnaire (selecting items from the initial set of satisfaction items which will compose your measure).

DETERMINING QUESTIONS OR ITEMS

Let's start with an example of an organization that would like to develop a customer satisfaction questionnaire. Suppose that the organization, in an attempt to gauge how well it services its customers, includes these requests in questionnaire:

1. Please rate the availability of the service.
2. Please rate the responsiveness of the staff.
3. Please rate the professionalism of the staff.

These three requests were obviously designed to measure three customer requirements, *availability of service, responsiveness of service*, and *professionalism of service*.

Although these customer requirements may be meaningful and valid service characteristics, there are problems with the requests. There is ambiguity in the phrases; "availability" and "responsiveness" might be interpreted differently by different people. As a result, responses to these questions will reflect this ambiguity. To illustrate how different people may have differing definitions for the same word, I asked 10 people to tell me the meaning of "some" using a number. Their answers ranged from "three" to "seven."

Similarly, if you ask your customers to indicate how satisfied they are with the *availability of service* they received, they may have different definitions of the word "availability" and thus are thinking of different things when they respond. Subsequently, it would be difficult to interpret customers' responses. To avoid this problem, our customer satisfaction questionnaire should use more specific statements which would leave less room for varying interpretations. Some statements that could more clearly describe "availability" include:

1. The merchant was available to schedule me at a good time.
2. I could get an appointment with the merchant at a time I desired.
3. My appointment was at a convenient time.

Availability is now defined more precisely in terms of scheduling and appointment time. Thus, responses to each of these items are more definitive than responses to the previous items. In addition, all three of these items still reflect the customer requirement of *availability of service*.

When we use more specific statements, the questionnaire provides specific feedback concerning organizational and staff performance. For example, the questionnaire in the first example with its use of the term "availability" may indicate that customers are not satisfied with the availability of service. Knowing that the customers are not satisfied, however, does little to help the organization pinpoint how to accomplish improvements. If the organization used more specific items (as in the second example), it would know precisely how to increase customers' level of satisfaction with the customer requirement of *availability of service*.

In summary, when developing questionnaires to assess customer satisfaction with a given product or service, we must ensure that our questions are not ambiguous. Using specific statements in questionnaires will enhance the information gained, because responses from customers mean the same thing across customers (no differing definitions) and responses will provide more specific feedback on ways to improve the service or product.

Satisfaction items revisited

We would like the questions in our questionnaire to be specific. The next step would be to determine what questions or statements to include. Recall that in Chapter 2, the critical incident technique includes the creation of satisfaction items. These can be used as items in the questionnaire. Satisfaction items related to the banking industry from Table 2.1 are presented in Table 4.1.

Satisfaction items can also provide indirect help by aiding the generation of new items for the questionnaire. This process entails rewriting the satisfaction items so that they reflect a neutral statement (neither positive nor negative) rather than a declarative statement. These items, however, are still specific in their content. These items (using the banking industry) appear in Table 4.2.

The items, either satisfaction items or items generated from them, are specific enough to be of value for feedback purposes. Instead of indicating only that customers are satisfied or dissatisfied with the level of profession-

1. I waited a short period of time before I was helped.
2. The service started promptly when I arrived.
3. The teller handled transactions in a short period of time.
4. The teller took a long time to complete my transaction.
5. The financial consultant was available to schedule me at a good time.
6. My appointment with the financial consultant was at a convenient time.
7. The teller talked to me in a pleasant way.
8. The teller was very personable.
9. The teller carefully listened to me when I was requesting a transaction.
10. The teller knew how to handle the transactions.
11. The quality of the way the teller treated me was high.
12. The way the teller treated me met my expectations.
13. I am satisfied with the way the merchant treated me.

TABLE 4.1 Satisfaction items from Table 2.1

1. Period of time waited before I was helped
2. Promptness of service when I arrived
3. Length of time of the transaction
4. Time to complete my transaction
5. Availability of financial consultant to schedule me for an appointment
6. Convenience of my appointment with the financial consultant
7. Way in which the teller talked to me
8. Way in which the teller conducted the transaction
9. Way in which the teller listened to me when I was requesting a transaction
10. Knowledge of teller in handling the transactions
11. The quality of the way the teller treated me
12. Overall quality of the visit
13. The way I was treated

TABLE 4.2 New items generated from original satisfaction items

alism of the service, these items can specify exactly why customers are satisfied or dissatisfied (items 7 through 10). In addition to studying the specific feedback these satisfaction items offer, we can calculate a general index of the *professionalism* customer requirement by combining the responses of items 7 to 10. We can also calculate indices for other quality dimensions or customer requirements using specific satisfaction items: *responsiveness* (items 1 and 2); *speed of transaction* (items 3 and 4); *availability* (items 5 and 6); and *overall satisfaction with service* (items 11 through 13). We can then determine the reliability of these summary scores using the reliability estimate formulae in Chapter 3.

The quality dimension development process also resulted in statements that could be included in the questionnaire. Recall that these statements also describe specific instances of the service or product that defined their respective quality dimensions. These statements are similar to the satisfaction items that result from the critical incident approach. Consequently, these statements can also be used directly in the customer satisfaction questionnaire.

CHARACTERISTICS OF GOOD ITEMS

Writing items for the questionnaire can be difficult. It is important that items possess certain characteristics. They should appear relevant to what you are trying to measure, assessing customer requirements established earlier in the process. Items that do not appear to measure anything relevant to the service or product might confuse the respondent, especially if the instructions indicate that the questionnaire is designed to assess the quality of the service or product.

Items should also be concise. Items that are too long can make the questionnaire too long and difficult to read. Discard superfluous words. An example of a long item is:

> The service person seemed to act in a very personable manner to me when I asked for service.

A concise item reflecting the same content would be:

> The service person was very personable.

Items should be unambiguous. The respondent should be able to understand precisely what the items are asking. Any ambiguity in the items can lead to equivocal responses. Try to avoid items that are vague and imprecise. For example, an item that might be ambiguous is:

> The transaction with the service provider was good.

This item does not reflect precisely why the service was good. Some respondents might interpret the item as assessing the promptness of the transaction, while others might think it assesses the service provider's professionalism. To avoid this confusion, we can write two items:

> The transaction took a short period of time.
> The service provider talked to me in a pleasant way.

Each of these items reflects two unambiguous thoughts, each representing one customer requirement.

A good item will contain only one thought. That is, the item should ask only one question. If an item asks more than one question, the respondent may be confused if he/she wants to respond affirmatively to one part of the question and negatively to the other part. A positive response to this type of item would indicate that the respondent agrees to both parts of the item. A negative response might indicate either that the respondent disagrees with one part of the item or that the respondent disagrees with both parts of the item. An example of a poor item is:

> The provider listened to me and took a short time to handle the transaction.

This item contains two parts, one dealing with how the provider listened to the customer and the other on whether the provider handled the transaction in a short amount of time. This item can be divided into two separate items:

The provider listened to me.
The provider took a short time to handle the transaction.

The fifth characteristic of a good item is that it should not contain a double negative. An example of an item with a double negative is:

The clerk was never not there when he/she was needed.

A better way to write this item is:

The clerk was there when he/she was needed.

In summary, a good item should appear relevant, be concise and unambiguous, contain only one thought, and not contain double negatives. Items with these characteristics offer respondents clear and simple questions to which to respond. They lead to a questionnaire that is easy to read and complete.

Although the items are an important part of the questionnaire, the response format of the items can also influence the quality of the responses obtained. The following section discusses response formats.

RESPONSE FORMATS

The second step of scale construction will be to select a response format for the questionnaire. A response format determines how customers can respond to the items on the questionnaire. The choice of a response format is an extremely important step in the development process since the response format determines how the data from the questionnaire can be used. This importance will become more clear in Chapter 5.

There are several possible response formats or scaling methods for questionnaires. These scaling methods include Thurstone's method of equal-appearing intervals (Thurstone, 1929), Guttman's scalogram approach (Guttman, 1950), and the Likert scaling method (Likert, 1932), to name a few. Questionnaire development using either the Thurstone or Guttman approach is more laborious than the Likert method. In addition, scales developed using the Likert method yield higher reliability coefficients with fewer items than scales developed using the Thurstone method (Edwards and Kenney, 1946). Therefore, for the sake of simplicity and utility, I will not present the Thurstone or Guttman approaches. I will limit this discussion of response formats to two approaches, the checklist format and the Likert-type format. Several books discuss the other types of scaling procedures not presented here (Dawes, 1972; Fishbein, 1967; and Reckase, 1990).

Checklist format

The quality of a service or product can be quantified by the number of positive things said about it. The more positive things said about a service (or the fewer negative things said about it), the better the service. For each item in the questionnaire, the customers will be allowed to respond either "yes" or "no." Customers are asked to respond "yes" if the satisfaction item reflects the service or product they received and "no" if the item does not reflect the service or product they received. An example of a checklist format is included in Figure 4.1. The checklist format should be used only when the satisfaction items are being used as the items in the questionnaire. The benefit of the checklist method is the ease with which customers can respond to the items. Customers can easily indicate whether or not the item describes the service they received.

Please indicate whether or not each statement describes the service you received. Check Yes if the statement describes the service or No if the statement does not describe the service.

	Yes	No
1. I could get an appointment with the merchant at a time I desired.	___	___
2. The merchant was available to schedule me at a good time.	___	___
3. My appointment was at a convenient time for me.	___	___
4. The merchant was quick to respond when I arrived for my appointment.	___	___
5. The merchant immediately helped me when I entered the premises.	___	___
6. My appointment started promptly at the scheduled time.	___	___

FIGURE 4.1 Example questionnaire using a checklist response format

Likert-type format

The quality of the service or product can also be indexed by the strength of response toward each satisfaction item. The Likert-type format is designed to allow customers to respond in varying degrees to each item that describes the service or product. For example, although two customers may say that the item describes the service, one customer may want to indicate the item especially describes the service more so than does the other customer.

To allow customers to respond in varying degrees to each item, a Likert-type response format can be used. R. A. Likert (1932) developed a scaling procedure in which the scale represents a bipolar continuum. The low end represents a negative response while the high end represents a positive response. Some Likert-type formats appear in Table 4.3. Each represents a bipolar continuum.

We can use these response formats for a particular type of item. The first response format in Table 4.3 (the *agree* to *disagree* continuum) is used with satisfaction items. Recall that satisfaction items are declarative items which reflect specific good or bad aspects of the service or product. The response scale, therefore, should reflect whether the satisfaction item describes the service. Customers respond to each item in terms of how well that particular item describes the service they received. The quality of the service is then indexed by the extent to which the items describe the service received. An example of a questionnaire using this rating format appears in Figure 4.2.

Strongly Disagree 1	Disagree 2	Neither Agree nor Disagree 3	Agree 4	Strongly Agree 5
Very Dissatisfied 1	Dissatisfied 2	Neither Satisfied nor Dissatisfied 3	Satisfied 4	Very Satisfied 5
Very Poor 1	Poor 2	Neither Poor nor Good 3	Good 4	Very Good 5

TABLE 4.3 Examples of Likert-type response formats

Please indicate the extent to which you agree or disagree with the following statements about the service you received from [company name]. Circle the appropriate number using the scale below.

1—I Strongly Disagree with this statement (SD).
2—I Disagree with this statement (D).
3—I Neither agree nor disagree with this statement (N).
4—I Agree with this statement (A).
5—I Strongly Agree with this statement (SA).

	SD	D	N	A	SA
1. I could get an appointment with the merchant at a time I desired.	1	2	3	4	5
2. The merchant was available to schedule me at a good time.	1	2	3	4	5
3. My appointment was at a convenient time for me.	1	2	3	4	5
4. The merchant was quick to respond when I arrived for my appointment.	1	2	3	4	5
5. The merchant immediately helped me when I entered the premises.	1	2	3	4	5
6. My appointment started promptly at the scheduled time.	1	2	3	4	5

FIGURE 4.2 Questionnaire using a Likert-type response format

The second and third response formats in Table 4.3 (*dissatisfied-satisfied* or *poor-good* continua) can be used for items like those found in Table 4.2. Although these items still reflect specific aspects of the service, they are rather neutral. The response scale, therefore, should reflect the degree to which the items (aspects of service) are satisfying (or good) versus dissatisfying (or poor). The quality of the service is indexed by the degree to which people say they are satisfied with the service or the degree to which the service is rated as good. Examples of questionnaires using these rating formats appear in Figures 4.3 and 4.4.

Please indicate the extent to which you are satisfied or dissatisfied with the following aspects of the service you received from [company name]. Circle the appropriate number using the scale below

> 1 — I am Very Dissatisfied with this aspect (VD).
> 2 — I am Dissatisfied with this aspect (D).
> 3 — I am Neither satisfied nor dissatisfied with this aspect (N).
> 4 — I am Satisfied with this aspect (S).
> 5 — I am Very Satisfied with this aspect (VS).

	VD	D	N	S	VS
1. Appointment time with the merchant	1	2	3	4	5
2. Availability of merchant to schedule me at a good time	1	2	3	4	5
3. Convenience of my appointment	1	2	3	4	5
4. Responsiveness of the merchant when I arrived for my appointment	1	2	3	4	5
5. Promptness of the start time of my appointment	1	2	3	4	5

FIGURE 4.3 Questionnaire using a Likert-type response format of satisfaction continuum

Advantage of Likert-type format

The advantage of using the Likert-type format rather than the checklist format is reflected in the variability of scores that result from the scale. With the quality dimension represented in our questionnaire, we allow customers to express the degree of their opinion in the service or product they received rather than restricting them to a "yes" or "no" answer. From a statistical perspective, scales with two response options have less reliability than scales with five response options (Lissitz and Green, 1975). In addition, reliability seems to level off after five scale points, suggesting minimal incremental utility of using more than five scale points.

In addition, using the Likert-type format will still allow you to determine the percentage of positive and negative responses for a given item. You may do this by combining the responses on the ends of the scale (for example, combining Strongly Disagree with Disagree and combining

Please rate the extent to which the aspect of the service from [company name] was good or bad. Circle the appropriate number using the scale below.

1—Aspect of service was Very Poor (VP).
2—Aspect of service was Poor (P).
3—Aspect of service was Neither poor nor good (N).
4—Aspect of service was Good (G).
5—Aspect of service was Very Good (VG).

	VP	P	N	G	VG
1. Appointment time with the merchant	1	2	3	4	5
2. Availability of merchant to schedule me at a good time	1	2	3	4	5
3. Convenience of my appointment	1	2	3	4	5
4. Responsiveness of the merchant when I arrived for my appointment	1	2	3	4	5
5. Promptness of the start time of my appointment	1	2	3	4	5

FIGURE 4.4 Questionnaire using a Likert-type response format of goodness continuum

Strongly Agree with Agree). A response of 1 or 2 is now considered to be a response of 1, a response of 3 is considered to be a response of 2, and a response of 4 or 5 is now considered to be response of 3. We have transformed our five-point scale into a three-point scale. A score of 1 represents a negative response, while a score of 3 represents a positive response. This transformation, therefore, creates somewhat of a checklist format.

INTRODUCTIONS TO CUSTOMER SATISFACTION QUESTIONNAIRES

The next step is to write the introduction to the questionnaire. The introduction should be brief. It should explain the purpose of the questionnaire and provide instructions for completing the questionnaire.

Also, you might explain how the data will be used. Keep this in simple terms that are easily understandable. Usually the questionnaire is designed to assess the customers' level of satisfaction. In some circumstances, however, a questionnaire may be designed for a special research project. To the extent that the customers' knowledge of the purpose of the project does not influence their responses, you might explain the purpose of the project in the instructions. Inclusion of the purpose could increase customers' perceptions that their response is highly valued in obtaining information about the project, thus making them more likely to complete the questionnaire.

The introduction should tell how to complete the items and explain the scale to be used. It is imperative that these instructions match the type of response format in the questionnaire. When you use the agree-disagree continuum as the response format, the instruction should ask respondents to indicate the extent to which they agree or disagree with the statements in the questionnaire. When you use the satisfaction continuum as the response format, the instructions should ask respondents to indicate the extent to which they are satisfied.

I have been asked why some of the items in the questionnaires seem redundant. Customers may become irritated because they feel they are answering the same question over and over again. Therefore, you might want to include the reason for the similarity of some items. State that the questionnaire was designed to include multiple items so that you obtain a more accurate assessment of your customers' opinion. The inclusion of this point might not be necessary if the items in the questionnaire are not highly similar to each other. You might want to pilot-test the questionnaire to see if respondents comment about the apparent redundancy of items.

An example of an introduction for a questionnaire using the agree-disagree continuum is:

> To better serve you, we would like to know your opinion of the quality of our service at [name of company or department]. You recently received service from our company [or department]. Please indicate the extent to which you agree or disagree with the following statements about the service you received from the staff. Circle the appropriate number using the scale below. Some statements are similar to one another to ensure that we accurately determine your opinion concerning our service.

1 — I Strongly Disagree with this statement (SD).

2 — I Disagree with this statement (D).

3 — I Neither agree nor disagree with this statement (N).

4 — I Agree with this statement (A).

5 — I Strongly Agree with this statement (SA).

This introduction includes the purpose of the questionnaire and instructions for completing the questions. Also, the introduction explains the purpose of using multiple items which are similar to each other.

ITEM SELECTION

Step four in the questionnaire construction process requires selecting the items to be used in the final questionnaire. Item selection might be warranted if the critical incidents technique resulted in a large number of satisfaction items. For example, if the critical incidents technique resulted in four quality dimensions each containing 10 items, it might not be practical to use all these items since it would be difficult to get our customers to complete a 40-item questionnaire. In this situation, we might want to select the best items from the original set to create a smaller, yet equally effective, customer satisfaction questionnaire. If the ratio of satisfaction items to quality dimensions is small (2:1 or less), we might not want to conduct any item selection procedure. Excluding items from an already small set could result in a customer satisfaction questionnaire with low reliability.

I will present two methods of item selection that will help you select the satisfaction items to include in the customer satisfaction questionnaire. The first method is based on human judgment, and the second is based on mathematical indices.

Judgmental item selection

One way to select items to use your best judgment. For your final customer satisfaction questionnaire, try to include items that best represent customers' requirements. The most critical element of this process is examining the similarity of items within a given quality dimension or customer requirement. Because the goal is to select items that best represent a particular dimension (customer satisfaction or various dimensions of customer requirements), these items should be somewhat similar to each other. If the items obtained from the critical incidents technique are all good, however, selecting the best items might be rather difficult.

One way to select the best satisfaction items—those that clearly reflect the quality dimension—is to have two people independently select a specified number of satisfaction items. Those chosen by both people will be retained. If there is low agreement, it is possible that all satisfaction items are equally good indicators of the underlying quality dimension; as a result, people cannot make a distinction between the items, and the low agreement is due to chance factors.

If there is no agreement in selected items, another method is to use a random selection process. If all the satisfaction items are judged to be equally good indicators of the quality dimensions, then any randomly selected set of satisfaction items from the original list will be a representative sample of items from the entire list. Another method is to select either every odd or every even numbered satisfaction item from the full list.

Mathematical item selection

Another method of selecting items is to administer all items generated from the critical incidents approach to some actual customers. After these customers complete the questionnaire, conduct item analysis on the data. Item analysis is a catch-all phrase which includes such processes as correlational analysis and factor analysis. You may conduct these statistical techniques to select the best items (those that have equal means and are highly interrelated). These statistical procedures require the help of an expert in questionnaire development. The following section of this chapter illustrates one approach that can be used in item selection.

Statistical procedures such as these will allow you to select which items to retain for your final measure of customer satisfaction. Although this approach is more complex than judgmental item selection, you achieve the invaluable payback of knowing your final questionnaire is statistically reliable; items retained as a result of the item analysis will be, by design, mathematically sound. The general goal in the selection of items is to retain items that differentiate between customers who are dissatisfied and those who are satisfied and drop items that do not. That is, the items should be able to discriminate between varying levels of customer satisfaction. Items on which highly satisfied and highly dissatisfied customers score the same are not very useful. Item analysis will allow us to identify those items that can discriminate between varying levels of satisfaction.

Item-total correlations. Item-total correlations are correlations between an item and the overall dimension score to which that item belongs (not including the one item being correlated). For example, if we had three items, each measuring the same quality dimension, we would calculate three item-total correlations: 1) item 1 correlated with the composite of items 2 and 3; 2) item 2 correlated with the composite of items 1 and 3; and 3) item 3 correlated with the composite of items 1 and 2. This type of correlation will tell you the extent to which each item is linked to the overall dimension score with which it should be highly linked. The criterion for a cutoff for a correlation coefficient varies depending on the purpose of the measure being developed. When developing a general type

Overall score
(minus item being correlated)

Item 1   r = .67

Item 2   r = .55

Item 3   r = .23

Item 4   r = .59

Item 5   r = .77

FIGURE 4.5 Hypothetical results of item-total correlations of items designed to measure perception of professionalism

of measure, you would use less stringent criteria compared to a measure designed to assess a more specific attitude (Likert, 1932). An important requirement is that the overall score of the measure be reliable.

As an example, we might have five items we want to combine into an overall score of *professionalism*. We must ensure that combining the five items make sense. If all the items are designed to measure the same dimension (perception of professionalism), then all items for that dimension should be positively related to each other, and we would expect to see high item-total correlations. Let's say we used the questionnaire on 100 customers and calculated five item-total correlation coefficients, one for each item. The results of a hypothetical item-total correlation analysis appear in Figure 4.5. We see that item 3 is not highly correlated with a composite of the remaining four items and might be dropped from the questionnaire. The remaining items show relatively high item-total correlations with the composite score of the remaining items. The results suggest that it would make sense to combine items 1, 2, 4, and 5 to obtain an overall score of *professionalism*.

The low correlation between item 3 and the remaining items could be due to several things. One possibility of why an item demonstrates a low correlation with its subscale might be that it is poorly written. For example, it could include two thoughts rather than one. Therefore, some respondents might want to respond favorably to one part of the item and unfavorably to the other part of the item. The item may have to be rewritten to reflect only one thought or divided into two separate items.

Another possibility is that a particular item measures some other customer requirement than what was originally thought. For the example above, we could calculate a correlation between item 3 and the other customer requirements. If item 3 does show a high correlation with another customer requirement, perhaps it should not be dropped from the questionnaire but, instead, included in the summary score for that particular customer requirement to which it is highly linked.

Another possibility is that the item represents a different customer requirement than those included in the questionnaire. An item may not correlate highly with any of the customer requirements. It could be that we failed to establish an important customer requirement in our clustering of critical incidents. This correlational approach could address such errors of omission. When this situation arises, perhaps we could write more items to reflect the content of that particular item. Subsequently, we could re-administer the revised questionnaire (with the new items) to conduct additional item analysis. If the new items are representative of that lone item, then that lone item should now correlate highly with the new items, thus forming a new customer requirement scale.

Group differences. Another mathematical item selection strategy employs the comparison of two groups of respondents (Likert, 1932). This procedure is also conducted after respondents have completed the questionnaire. Within each subscale (e.g., *availability* or *timeliness*), we select two groups of people, each group representing the extreme of the attitude measured by a particular scale. Usually, the top and bottom 10 percent are selected, based on their overall score for the particular subscale. Next, for each group, we calculate means for each item. Then we calculate a difference score for each item, subtracting the mean of the lower extreme group from the mean of the higher extreme group.

For each item we obtain a difference score. This difference score reflects how much a particular item was able to discriminate between the two groups on an attitude the item was designed to measure. The higher the difference score, the higher the discrimination. If an item does not differentiate between the two groups, then we would obtain a difference score of 0. These items are dropped from the questionnaire. For items that are positively phrased (higher score means higher level of the attitude), we select items that have a large positive difference score. For those items that are negatively phrased (higher score means lower level of the attitude), we select items that have a large negative difference score.

The indices used in the item-total correlation procedure (item-total correlation) and the group differences procedure (difference score) have been shown to be highly correlated (Likert, 1932). This suggests that both procedures will result in similar outcomes with respect to the inclusion of items in the final form of the questionnaire.

Factor analysis. Another statistical technique of item selection, often used in conjunction with item-total correlations, is factor analysis. This technique (see Appendix K) will demonstrate which items are more highly related to the underlying dimension they are designed to measure.

Factor analysis is a highly specialized form of analysis. It is beyond the scope of this book to provide you with exact procedures for the selection of items. However, here are some general guidelines. It is essential that items within each scale load on a single factor if the items are to be used in a composite score. When an item loads highly on a different factor than the one for which it was intended, this suggests that the item might best be combined with items with which it is highly related. When an item does not load highly on any factor, this suggests that the item does not discriminate between high and low groups on the attitudes that are measured with the items in the current questionnaire.

An advantage of using factor analysis is the identification of underlying constructs (customer requirements) being measured by the items in the questionnaire. Also, factor analysis allows us to determine which customer requirement each item is measuring. A disadvantage of factor analysis is that it requires a large number of respondents to complete questionnaires if the results are to be reliable. The number of respondents should be 5 to 10 times the number of items in the questionnaire. For example, if the questionnaire contains 20 items, the factor analysis should be conducted using the responses of 100 to 200 people.

Factor analysis has been used in applied research. For example, Parasuraman, Zeithaml, and Berry (1988) used factor analysis in developing a service quality questionnaire. The goal of the research was to develop a reliable scale which assesses various components of service quality. The authors present the results of the exploratory factor analysis of responses to 97 items.

On the basis of the factor analysis, the authors selected items that were good indicators of underlying dimensions. They also presented the results of the factor analysis, which included the number of factors as well as the factor pattern matrix (after rotation). This article presents an excellent example of the use of factor analysis in developing customer satisfaction questionnaires.

Mathematical item selection is usually used in the initial stages of questionnaire development. Even if you use the judgmental item selection process, you may conduct item analysis on the retained items (after customers have completed them) to determine if the items chosen constitute a reliable scale. Table 4.4 presents the chronological use of item analysis in the selection of items when using either the mathematical item selection or the judgmental item selection process.

JUDGMENTAL ITEM SELECTION	MATHEMATICAL ITEM SELECTION
1. Select small set of items using judgmental criteria or random selection.	1. Place all satisfaction items in the questionnaire.
2. Place this set of satisfaction items in the questionnaire.	2. Use questionnaire on customers.
3. Use questionnaire on customers.	3. Conduct item analysis to determine which items to retain for final questionnaire (need sufficient sample size of approximately five people per item if factor analysis will be used).
4. Conduct item analysis to determine if these items measure quality dimensions.	4. Examine outcome of item analysis and select good items for final version of questionnaire.
5. Examine outcome of item analysis to retain good items.	5. Use final version of the questionnaire.
6. Results may indicate entire questionnaire revision (if items do not measure the underlying dimensions).	

TABLE 4.4 The use of item analysis in judmental item selection and mathematical item selection

SUMMARY

Items in the customer satisfaction questionnaire should be relevant, concise, and unambiguous. They should also be written clearly to reflect only one thought and avoid double negatives. Also, the introduction provides the purpose of the questionnaire as well as instructions for completing it.

This chapter presented two response formats that can be used in questionnaires. A checklist format allows customers to indicate whether a particular item represents the service or product. A Likert-type format allows customers to further distinguish their response beyond what is

STEPS	IMPORTANT ISSUES
1. Generate items for questionnaire.	■ Select items from satisfaction item list.
	■ Write items based on satisfaction items.
2. Ensure items are written appropriately.	■ Items should appear relevant to what you are trying to measure.
	■ Items should be concise.
	■ Items should be unambiguous.
	■ Items should contain only one thought (items ask only one question).
	■ Items should not contain double negatives.
3. Select response format for items.	■ Checklist format
	■ Likert-type format
4. Write introduction to questionnaire.	■ State the purpose of the questionnaire.
	■ State instructions on how to complete the questionnaire.
5. Select representative sample of items.	■ Items within each quality dimension should be similar in content to each other.
a. could use judgmental item selection to select items	■ Use multiple judges to select the items.
b. could use mathematical item selection to select items	■ Use item-total correlations or group differences approach in selecting items.
	■ could also use factor analysis
6. Evaluate the retained items.	■ Calculate reliability of the scales within questionnaire using split-half method or Cronbach's estimate.

TABLE 4.5 Guidelines in the development of questionnaires

allowed by the checklist format. The choice between these two types of formats depends on the type of data desired from the questionnaire.

Also, this chapter outlined two procedures used when selecting items for the customer satisfaction questionnaire. The judgmental procedure can be useful when the initial items are all good items. If you are using the mathematical approach, consult somebody conversant in these mathematical procedures when you attempt to select items. Mathematical item selection is designed to select items that are statistically sound.

Table 4.5 outlines the general steps to follow in questionnaire development. Each step is accompanied by various methods that are used for each step as well as other important issues to consider. This table is designed to summarize and highlight the important points in the chapter and can be used as a checklist when developing the questionnaire.

Five

USING CUSTOMER SATISFACTION QUESTIONNAIRES

This chapter will present five examples of customer satisfaction question-naires and outline some specific things you can do with data derived from them. I will demonstrate how you can present and summarize data, as well as determine which of the customer requirements is most important in determining customer satisfaction. Also, I will demonstrate how the data can be applied to traditional quality improvement methodologies, including control charting techniques.

EXAMPLES OF CUSTOMER SATISFACTION QUESTIONNAIRES

Previous chapters outlined some guidelines and issues to address when developing customer satisfaction questionnaires. This section will present five customer satisfaction questionnaires: one based on the results of the quality dimension development process applied to the soft-ware industry, another based on the general quality dimensions applied to a facilities organization within a company, and three based on the results of the critical incidents applied to the banking and automobile industries and the internal statistical department in Chapter 2. These will allow you to see the structure of a questionnaire, designed on the basis of the guidelines presented in earlier chapters.

Software Quality

The response format for each questionnaire is the Likert-type format using the agree-disagree continuum. (The checklist format could have been used also.) The questionnaire for the software industry appears in Figure 5.1. Although there are 20 items in the questionnaire, this ques-tionnaire was designed to represent 10 dimensions of software quality.

To better serve you, we would like to know your opinion of the quality of our software. Please indicate the extent to which you agree or disagree with the following statements about the software [name of software]. Circle the appropriate number using the scale below. Some of the statements are similar to one another to ensure that we accurately determine your opinion concerning the software.

1—I Strongly Disagree with this statement (SD).
2—I Disagree with this statement (D).
3—I Neither agree nor disagree with this statement (N).
4—I Agree with this statement (A).
5—I Strongly Agree with this statement (SA).

	SD	D	N	A	SA
1. I am able to complete my job with this software.	1	2	3	4	5
2. The software meets my specifications in getting my job done.	1	2	3	4	5
3. I am able to perform functions with precision.	1	2	3	4	5
4. The software allows me to perform functions accurately.	1	2	3	4	5
5. I was able to learn about the output from programs in a short amount of time.	1	2	3	4	5
6. The output of the programs is easy to understand.	1	2	3	4	5
7. Fixing an error in the operational program is easy.	1	2	3	4	5
8. Locating an error in the operational program is easy.	1	2	3	4	5
9. The testing of the program required a short amount of time.	1	2	3	4	5
10. Testing the program to ensure it performed functions was easy.	1	2	3	4	5
11. Transferring the program between different hardware configurations is easy.	1	2	3	4	5

FIGURE 5.1 Example of a customer satisfaction questionnaire for the software industry

	SD	D	N	A	SA
12. I am able to transfer programs between different software environments with little problem.	1	2	3	4	5
13. Coupling one system to another is easy.	1	2	3	4	5
14. The software allows for simple coupling between systems.	1	2	3	4	5
15. Communicating between software components is simple.	1	2	3	4	5
16. I am able to communicate between software components easily.	1	2	3	4	5
17. I am able to modify the operational program with little effort.	1	2	3	4	5
18. Changing the operational program is easy to do.	1	2	3	4	5
19. I am very happy with the software.	1	2	3	4	5
20. The software meets my expectations.	1	2	3	4	5

Additional comments:

FIGURE 5.1 continued

Therefore, we could conceivably derive 10 scores, each score representing the quality for a particular dimension. The dimensions and their items are:

1. *correctness* (items 1 and 2)
2. *reliability* (items 3 and 4)
3. *usability* (items 5 and 6)
4. *maintainability* (items 7 and 8)
5. *testability* (items 9 and 10)
6. *portability* (items 11 and 12)

To better serve you, we would like to know your opinion of the quality of our service and products. You recently received help from Facilities department. Please indicate the extent to which you agree or disagree with the following statements about the service you received from the staff of Facilities. Circle the appropriate number using the scale below. Some of the statements are similar to one another to ensure that we accurately determine your opinion concerning our service.

1—I Strongly Disagree with this statement (SD).
2—I Disagree with this statement (D).
3—I Neither agree nor disagree with this statement (N).
4—I Agree with this statement (A).
5—I Strongly Agree with this statement (SA).

	SD	D	N	A	SA
1. I could get help from Facilities when I needed.	1	2	3	4	5
2. The Facilities staff was there when they were needed.	1	2	3	4	5
3. I could arrange convenient meeting times with the staff.	1	2	3	4	5
4. Facilities was quick to respond when I asked for help.	1	2	3	4	5
5. Facilities immediately helped me if needed.	1	2	3	4	5
6. I waited a short period of time to get help after I asked for it.	1	2	3	4	5
7. Facilities completed the job when expected.	1	2	3	4	5
8. Facilities did not meet my deadline(s).	1	2	3	4	5
9. Facilities staff finished their responsibilities within the stated time-frame.	1	2	3	4	5
10. The staff conducted themselves in a professional manner.	1	2	3	4	5
11. The staff was courteous.	1	2	3	4	5
12. The staff cared about what I had to say.	1	2	3	4	5

FIGURE 5.2 Example of a customer satisfaction questionnaire for a facilities organization

	SD	D	N	A	SA
13. The quality of the way Facilities treated me is high.	1	2	3	4	5
14. The way Facilities treated me met my expectations.	1	2	3	4	5
15. I am satisfied with the way Facilities treated me.	1	2	3	4	5
16. The quality of the final job Facilities provided is high.	1	2	3	4	5
17. The job met my expectations.	1	2	3	4	5
18. I am satisfied with the job that Facilities provided.	1	2	3	4	5

Additional Comments:

FIGURE 5.2 Continued

7. *interoperability* (items 13 and 14)

8. *intra-operability* (items 15 and 16)

9. *flexibility* (items 17 and 18)

10. *overall satisfaction* (items 19 and 20)

Additional analysis (factor analysis) might reveal a smaller subset of dimensions after customers complete the questionnaire. Customers may not be able to distinguish between nine separate dimensions of software quality.

Facilities department

The next questionnaire is presented in Figure 5.2. This example illustrates the use of customer satisfaction questionnaires for internal customers (customers within the same company as the provider). The questionnaire was based on the general service quality dimensions presented by Kennedy and Young (1989). The items reflect each of the quality dimensions. The quality dimensions and their respective items are:

1. *availability of service* (items 1 through 3)

2. *responsiveness of service* (items 4 through 6)

3. *timeliness of service* (items 7 through 9)

4. *professionalism of service* (items 10 through 12)

5. *overall satisfaction with service* (items 13 through 15)

6. *overall satisfaction with product* (items 16 through 18)

Although this questionnaire might represent a comprehensive examination of the general service quality dimensions, there still may be other quality dimensions specific to any one facilities organization that should be included in the questionnaire. Therefore, more items might be needed to more fully represent the entire range of possible quality dimensions.

Banking industry

The next questionnaire is presented in Figure 5.3 and represents the banking industry. One of its statements has a negative connotation (item 4). It is possible that some items in any questionnaire will be phrased negatively. Due to this "negativity," a score of 5 for this statement reflects poor service while a score of 1 reflects good service. Therefore, adding the scores from this statement (item 4) to scores from item 3 would be incorrect. Due to the negativity of item 4, we would reverse the scores for this statement so that a score of 1 on the original scale becomes 5, 2 on the original scale becomes 4, 4 on the original scale becomes 2, and 1 on the original scale becomes 5. Once we have completed the transformation, averaging the response of items 3 and 4 is appropriate.

You could conceivably derive 13 scores for each customer based on this questionnaire (one score for each of the 13 items). This questionnaire, however, was designed to assess four quality dimensions and one dimension labeled *overall customer satisfaction*. Therefore, some items would be combined to get measures of customers' perception of various quality dimensions. The dimensions and their corresponding items are:

1. *responsiveness of service* (items 1 and 2)

2. *speed of transaction* (items 3 and 4)

3. *availability of service* (items 5 and 6)

4. *professionalism* (items 7 through 10)

5. *overall satisfaction with service* (items 11 through 13)

Automobile industry

The next customer satisfaction questionnaire is presented in Figure 5.4 and represents the automobile industry. The introduction to this questionnaire is addressed to the person who just drove a particular car. This demonstrates a particular use of customer satisfaction questionnaires: the comparison of cars from different automobile manufacturers. This questionnaire might be used by an independent customer research group conducting a study comparing different cars. The full experimental design of the study would be complex and will not be presented here. The general design of the study, however, would be to allow customers to drive all the cars being studied. After each drive, the person completes the questionnaire to indicate his or her perception of the car's quality. Subsequently, the data can be used to make direct comparisons between the automobiles.

Again, scores derived from this questionnaire should reflect dimensions being measured by the various items. The dimensions and their corresponding items are:

1. *interior quality* (items 1 through 3)

2. *instrumentation* (items 4 and 5)

3. *drivability* (items 6 through 8)

4. *overall satisfaction with auto* (items 9 through 11)

Statistical support department

The questionnaire for the statistical support department is presented in Figure 5.5. This questionnaire would likely be distributed to the customers after the completion of a project. The customer would answer the questionnaire with respect to that particular project. This questionnaire was designed to assess five customer requirements as well as overall customer satisfaction:

1. *statistical support* (items 1 through 3)

2. *enthusiasm* (items 4 and 5)

3. *final written report* (items 6 and 7)

4. *responsiveness* (items 8 and 9)

5. *project management* (items 10 and 11)

6. *overall satisfaction with service* (items 12 and 13)

To better serve you, we would like to know your opinion of the quality of our service and products. Please indicate the extent to which you agree or disagree with the following statements about the service you received from [company name]. Circle the appropriate number using the scale below. Some of the statements are similar to one another to ensure that we accurately determine your opinion concerning our service.

1 – I Strongly Disagree with this statement (SD).
2 – I Disagree with this statement (D).
3 – I Neither agree nor disagree with this statement (N).
4 – I Agree with this statement (A).
5 – I Strongly Agree with this statement (SA).

	SD	D	N	A	SA
1. I waited a short period of time before I was helped.	1	2	3	4	5
2. The service started immediately when I arrived.	1	2	3	4	5
3. The teller handled transactions in a short period of time.	1	2	3	4	5
4. The teller took a long time to complete my transaction.	1	2	3	4	5
5. The financial consultant was available to schedule me at a good time.	1	2	3	4	5
6. My appointment with the financial consultant was at a convenient time.	1	2	3	4	5
7. The teller talked to me in a pleasant way.	1	2	3	4	5
8. The teller was very personable.	1	2	3	4	5
9. The teller carefully listened to me when I was requesting a transaction.	1	2	3	4	5
10. The teller knew how to handle the transactions.	1	2	3	4	5
11. The quality of way the teller treated me was high.	1	2	3	4	5

FIGURE 5.3 Example of a customer satisfaction questionnaire for the banking industry

	SD	D	N	A	SA
12. The way the teller treated me met my expectations.	1	2	3	4	5
13. I am satisfied with the way the teller treated me.	1	2	3	4	5

Additional comments:

FIGURE 5.3 continued

USES OF CUSTOMER SATISFACTION QUESTIONNAIRES

Next, I will present four uses of customer satisfaction questionnaires: 1) summarizing data with descriptive statistics; 2) determining the most important customer requirement; 3) control chart techniques to track the quality of the product or service over time; and 4) the comparison of customer satisfaction between companies.

SUMMARY INDICES

The presentation of the data is an important issue. The quality of the data obtained from the customer satisfaction questionnaire depends on the way in which the data are summarized and presented. A reliable questionnaire will be of little practical use if the data cannot be understood. This part of the chapter will present some summary indices of a sample of data and will demonstrate how data can be presented.

One way to summarize the data is to use summary indices that describe important aspects of the data. Summary indices that describe a sample of data are called statistics (Appendix E).

The statistics that summarize the elements in a data set reflect the central tendency of the data and the dispersion of the data. Three statistics are the arithmetic average or mean, the variance, and the standard deviation. The mean indicates the central tendency of data, while the latter two describe the spread of the data. The formula for the arithmetic average is $(\Sigma x_i)/n$. The Σ notation (called sigma) indicates summation of the variables, and n equals the number of elements in the data set. For the

We would like to know your opinion of the quality of the automobile you just drove. Please indicate the extent to which you agree or disagree with the following statements. Circle the appropriate number using the scale below. Some of the statements are similar to one another to ensure that we accurately determine your opinion concerning the automobile.

> 1 — I Strongly Disagree with this statement (SD).
> 2 — I Disagree with this statement (D).
> 3 — I Neither agree nor disagree with this statement (N).
> 4 — I Agree with this statement (A).
> 5 — I Strongly Agree with this statement (SA).

	SD	D	N	A	SA
1. The seating position was very comfortable.	1	2	3	4	5
2. The visibility through the window was good.	1	2	3	4	5
3. The inside of the car was noisy.	1	2	3	4	5
4. The instrumentation panel was simple to understand.	1	2	3	4	5
5. The instrumentation panel was clearly visible from the driving seat.	1	2	3	4	5
6. The car stopped smoothly when I applied the brakes.	1	2	3	4	5
7. The car vibrated at high speeds.	1	2	3	4	5
8. The car handled corners well.	1	2	3	4	5
9. I enjoyed driving the car.	1	2	3	4	5
10. I liked the overall driving experience of the car.	1	2	3	4	5
11. The drive was excellent.	1	2	3	4	5

Additional comments:

FIGURE 5.4 Example of a customer satisfaction questionnaire for the automobile industry

present equation, sigma indicates that all the observations going into the calculation of the mean will be added together. This sum is then divided by the number of observations. The resulting number is the mean. The equation for the mean can also be expressed as:

$$\bar{x} = \frac{x_1 + x_2 + \ldots + x_n}{n}$$

where n equals the number of elements in the data set.

The formula for the variance is:

$$s^2 = \frac{\sum_{i=1}^{n} (x_i - \bar{x})^2}{n - 1}$$

where n equals the number of elements in the sample.

The sample standard deviation, which is also a measure of variability, is the square root of the sample variance.

Presentation of data

I will use a hypothetical example to illustrate how data can be presented. A company used a customer satisfaction questionnaire to gauge the level of service it provided. This questionnaire was designed to measure several customer requirements and overall customer satisfaction. A portion of these items appears in Figure 5.6. Items 1 through 3 measure *availability of service*; items 4 through 6 measure *responsiveness of service*; and items 7 through 9 measure *overall customer satisfaction*.

The company solicited responses from customers. Data for 20 customers are presented in Table 5.1. It is apparent, even from this small set of data, that examination of the raw data does not reveal much information. The table looks like a series of unrelated numbers. We need to summarize the data in a clear, concise format to help us interpret the important findings. To do so, we have calculated the average and standard deviation for each item.

Also, summary scores for the two customer requirement categories are calculated, as well as a summary score for *overall customer satisfaction*. These scores are the average of the items within that given dimension. These summary scores can provide a more general measure of service quality and are particularly useful for presentations to upper management. We have calculated reliability estimates (Cronbach's alpha estimate) for each dimension. These estimates are essential, because they indicate the quality of the summary scores.

To better serve you, we would like to know your opinion of the quality of our service and products. You recently received help from [department name]. Please indicate the extent to which you agree or disagree with the following statements about the service you received from the staff. Circle the appropriate number using the scale below. Some of the statements are similar to one another to ensure that we accurately determine your opinion concerning our service.

1—I Strongly Disagree with this statement (SD).
2—I Disagree with this statement (D).
3—I Neither agree nor disagree with this statement (N).
4—I Agree with this statement (A).
5—I Strongly Agree with this statement (SA).

	SD	D	N	A	SA
1. The staff person explained the statistical tests in understandable words.	1	2	3	4	5
2. The statistical analyses were thorough.	1	2	3	4	5
3. The staff understood my software requirements.	1	2	3	4	5
4. The staff person was always willing to help.	1	2	3	4	5
5. The staff person went out of his/her way to help.	1	2	3	4	5
6. The written report was sufficiently detailed.	1	2	3	4	5
7. The written report contained what I needed.	1	2	3	4	5
8. The staff person completed the job quickly.	1	2	3	4	5
9. The staff person finished the project in the stated time frame.	1	2	3	4	5
10. The staff person planned out the entire project through its completion.	1	2	3	4	5
11. The staff person understood how much time the project required.	1	2	3	4	5
12. I am satisfied with the service I received.	1	2	3	4	5

FIGURE 5.5 Example of a customer satisfaction questionnaire for the an internal statistical support department

	SD	D	N	A	SA
13. The quality of the service met my expectations.	1	2	3	4	5

Additional comments:

FIGURE 5.5 continued

Summary

It is important that data from questionnaires be summarized in an understandable format. Often, the mean and standard deviations are used to summarize information in the data set. Summary scores for each dimension can provide general measures of the quality of the service or product.

IDENTIFY IMPORTANT CUSTOMER REQUIREMENTS

Suppose our service organization has developed a customer satisfaction questionnaire that assesses five quality dimensions and overall customer satisfaction, and we solicit responses from our customers. Also, suppose that the questionnaire results indicate that the average score for the five quality dimensions and overall customer satisfaction are roughly the same. In addition, our supervisor has given us the resources to increase service quality. Given this information, on which of the five quality dimensions should we apply the resources?

For this situation (and possibly for all situations), examining the satisfaction level for each dimension would be of little use, since the satisfaction levels are (or could be) the same across all dimensions. A better method would be to determine which quality dimension is most highly related to overall customer satisfaction. If our goal is to increase overall customer satisfaction, we should direct resources toward those dimensions which would increase overall customer satisfaction.

To determine which dimensions are closely linked with overall customer satisfaction, we could determine the extent to which each dimension is correlated with overall customer satisfaction. One way to deter-

Please indicate the extent to which you agree or disagree with the following statements concerning the service you received. Please circle your response for each question using the following scale.

1—I Strongly Disagree with this statement (SD).
2—I Disagree with this statement (D).
3—I Neither agree nor disagree with this statement (N).
4—I Agree with this statement (A).
5—I Strongly Agree with this statement (SA).

		SD	D	N	A	SA
1.	I could get an appointment with the merchant at a time I desired.	1	2	3	4	5
2.	The merchant was available to schedule me at a good time.	1	2	3	4	5
3.	My appointment was at a convenient time for me.	1	2	3	4	5
4.	The merchant was quick to respond when I arrived for my appointment.	1	2	3	4	5
5.	The merchant immediately helped me when I entered the premises.	1	2	3	4	5
6.	My appointment started promptly at the scheduled time.	1	2	3	4	5
7.	The quality of the way the merchant treated me was high.	1	2	3	4	5
8.	The way the merchant treated me met my expectations.	1	2	3	4	5
9.	Overall, I am satisfied with the service.	1	2	3	4	5

FIGURE 5.6 Example satisfaction items measuring two customer requirements and overall customer satisfaction

mine which quality dimension is most important would be simply to ask customers the extent to which each quality dimension is important in making them satisfied with the service. For example, each customer could rate the importance of each quality dimension in their satisfaction. For each dimension, we would calculate an average score of these rat-

	Satisfaction items								
Customer	1	2	3	4	5	6	7	8	9
1	5	4	5	3	4	4	3	4	3
2	3	2	3	5	4	5	4	4	4
3	4	5	5	3	2	2	3	3	4
4	3	2	3	4	3	4	4	5	4
5	3	3	3	4	4	4	3	3	3
6	4	4	5	4	5	4	4	5	4
7	3	4	2	4	3	3	3	2	3
8	5	4	5	4	4	4	5	4	5
9	3	2	3	4	3	4	4	4	3
10	3	4	3	4	4	4	3	4	3
11	5	5	5	5	5	5	5	5	5
12	4	4	4	3	3	4	4	4	4
13	4	4	5	5	5	4	4	4	5
14	2	2	3	4	4	5	3	3	2
15	4	5	5	4	4	3	4	3	3
16	5	4	5	5	5	5	4	4	4
17	3	4	3	5	4	4	4	4	4
18	3	2	4	3	3	4	2	2	2
19	5	4	3	4	5	4	3	3	4
20	3	3	3	4	3	3	4	4	4
Mean =	3.70	3.55	3.85	4.05	3.85	3.95	3.65	3.70	3.65
Standard Deviation =	0.92	1.05	1.04	0.69	0.88	0.76	0.75	0.87	0.88

Summary scores for customer requirements (reliability estimates in parentheses)

	Availability of Service (.85)	Responsiveness of Service (.81)	Overall Satisfaction (.88)
Mean =	3.70	3.95	3.67
Standard Deviation =	0.88	0.66	0.74

TABLE 5.1 Example data from 20 customers responding to a customer satisfaction questionnaire

ings. This average would indicate the level of importance of that particular dimension in satisfying the customers.

Research on human judgment, however, suggests that people are poor judges as to what information they think they use. A statistical model is better at predicting outcomes compared to judgmental models. One statistical approach is correlation analysis (see Appendix J).

After customers complete the customer satisfaction questionnaire, we would calculate scores for each quality dimension. Therefore, each customer would get a score on each of the quality dimensions represented on the customer satisfaction questionnaire, as well as a score for *overall satisfaction.*

After calculating scores, the next step would be to correlate each quality dimension with the *overall satisfaction* score. The correlations between each of the quality dimensions and overall customer satisfaction scores reflect the importance of each quality dimension in predicting overall customer satisfaction. The higher the correlation, the more important the quality dimension is in satisfying customers.

Here is an illustration of this method using quality dimensions associated with the banking industry. Suppose I calculated the correlations between each of the quality dimensions and overall customer satisfaction and found them to be $r = .50$ for *responsiveness of service, $r = .15$ for speed of transaction, $r = .25$ for availability of service*, and $r = .40$ for *professionalism.* These results reveal that both *responsiveness* and *professionalism* are important in determining *overall customer satisfaction.* As a result, resources would probably have their greatest effect on overall customer satisfaction if applied in these two areas.

Determination of important quality dimensions does not have to be confined to a single point in time. Even though current results indicate the most important quality dimensions are *responsiveness* and *professionalism*, other quality dimensions may come to the fore later. The relative ordering of customers' requirements or expectations may change over time. Thus, a continual determination of important customer requirements is necessary. Also, it is important to consider the effect of reliability on the correlation between variables (see Chapter 3). Recall that a statistically nonsignificant correlation between two variables might result from the unreliability of the scales. Therefore, you must determine the reliability of the scales.

Summary

Recall that all of the quality dimensions being assessed by the customer satisfaction questionnaire are, by design, important to customers. It is beneficial to understand which of these quality dimensions is most highly linked with overall customer satisfaction. This information is necessary when determining where to direct company resources. The best method is to collect data with the questionnaire and determine, through correlational analysis, the most important quality dimensions.

Interpretation of the correlations is reserved for those knowledgeable in statistics. Factors such as restriction in range of scores and collinearity of quality dimensions should be considered when determining which quality characteristic is most important in determining overall customer satisfaction. Also, calculation of correlation coefficients is only one way of determining the important dimensions. Another approach involves multiple regression analysis, which is a more sophisticated method of determining relationships between variables. For the interested reader, several statistics textbooks include these topics (Neter, Wasserman, and Kutner, 1985; Pedhazur, 1982).

Once we have identified these important quality dimensions, the next step is to track their level of quality. This is often done with the help of control charts. Next, I will present an overview of control chart techniques and discuss specific uses of these charts. A more comprehensive discussion of control charts and statistical process control methodologies is available elsewhere (Montgomery, 1985).

CONTROL CHARTS

Control charts represent various ways data can be charted. An example of a control chart appears in Figure 5.7. The control chart is a visual display of the overall service or product quality. In addition, control charts can display each of the quality characteristics. The ordinate (vertical axis) of the control chart represents the measurement of the overall quality dimension of a particular quality dimension. The abscissa (horizontal axis) represents either the sample number or time. The control chart includes a center line representing the average value of the quality dimensions over the entire range of samples. The chart also contains an upper control limit (UCL) and lower control limit (LCL) that run parallel with the center line.

There are general formulae for the control chart's center line, UCL, and LCL. Let's use Q to represent the sample statistic of the quality characteristic we are measuring. Let's indicate the mean of Q as $\bar{x}_Q$ and the variance of Q as $s^2_{(Q)}$. With these labels, the general formulae for the control charts are:

$$\text{UCL} = \bar{x}_Q + k\sqrt{s^2_{(Q)}}$$
$$\text{Center line} = \bar{x}_Q$$
$$\text{LCL} = \bar{x}_Q - k\sqrt{s^2_{(Q)}}$$

where k represents a constant used to determine the distance of the UCL and LCL from the center line. It is standard that k equal 3.0; therefore, 3 will be used in the remaining equations.

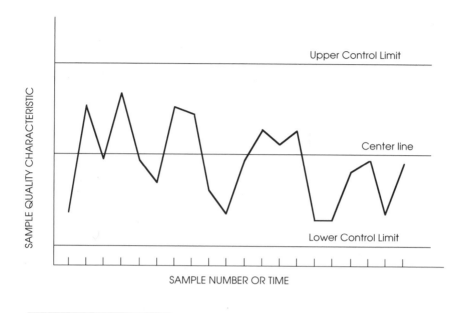

FIGURE 5.7 Example of a control chart

Interpretation of the control chart

Control charts can monitor the business processes that generate the data in the chart. Each data point in the control chart indicates how the process is running at a given time. Over time, because of natural variability inherent in the process, we expect that not all data points will fall on the center line. This natural variability is due to random causes referred to as uncontrollable factors. Under these conditions, we expect the data points will fall somewhere between the UCL and the LCL. When this pattern occurs, the process is said to be *in statistical control*.

There are additional sources of variability that will influence the output of the process. The variability from these other sources is usually larger than the natural variability and is due to events that represent a potential problem in the process when they occur. The sources of this extreme variability are referred to as *assignable causes*. Their presence is indicated by a data point falling outside the control limits (either above the UCL or below the LCL). When this pattern occurs, the process is said to be *out of control*. Using control charts helps us remove the source of this type of variability. Specific uses of control charts will be presented in examples later in the chapter.

Types of data

Quality dimension data can be categorized as attribute data and variable data. Attribute data is usually categorical. Measurements of quality characteristics are classified as either conforming to specifications or not conforming to specifications and divide occurrences into "nondefective" or "defective" categories, respectively.

Variable data is numerical. We can apply a unit of measurement (e.g., inches or minutes) to quality characteristics. Not only can we determine the number of nonconforming occurrences, we can also determine the degree to which an occurrence is not conforming to specifications.

The type of data that is gathered is often a function of the process being measured or the measurement tool used. As will be apparent later, data from customer satisfaction questionnaires can be used as either categorical data or variable data. We can apply either of the two types of data (attribute or variable) to control charts. Next, I will present some ways in which we can apply data from customer satisfaction questionnaires to control chart techniques.

CONTROL CHARTS FOR ATTRIBUTE DATA

Recall that we can allocate attribute data into categories (for example, categories of "defective" and "nondefective"). Two attribute control charts that apply are the p chart and the c chart.

The p chart

Quality of a service could be evident in the percentage of people who volunteer at least one negative response. A decrease in the percentage of these people indicates an increase in the quality of service. For any given sample of customers completing our questionnaire, we can calculate the percentage of people who gave at least one negative response. In a sense, this percentage represents the number of defects in our sample. The formula for this percentage is:

$$p_i = D_i / n_i$$

> where D_i is the number of people who gave at least one negative response for a given sample (i) and n_i is the sample size.

The percentage, p, is calculated for every sample. Given that the sample size is constant, we can create the control chart using the average of all ps. The formula for the UCL, center line, and LCL are:

$$UCL = \bar{p} + 3\sqrt{\frac{\bar{p}(1-\bar{p})}{n}}$$

Center line $= \bar{p}$

$$LCL = \bar{p} - 3\sqrt{\frac{\bar{p}(1-\bar{p})}{n}}$$

Example of the p chart

Using the customer satisfaction questionnaire for the banking industry (see figure 5.3), we would like to determine the percentage of customers who give at least one negative response about service they received from banking personnel. The bank is experiencing a high number of complaints related to banking personnel. A negative response occurs when the customer indicates he/she either Disagreed or Strongly Disagreed to a positively phrased satisfaction item (e.g., questions 2 and 3) or Agreed or Strongly Agreed to a negative satisfaction item (e.g., question 4). Data collected over 20 weeks appear in Table 5.2. Sample size for each of the 20 samples is 50.

The calculations of the UCL, center line, and LCL are:

$$UCL = .213 + 3(.0579) = .3867$$

Center line $= .213$

$$LCL = .213 - 3(.0579) = .0393$$

The resulting control chart appears in Figure 5.8. The plotted numbers for each sample represent the percentage of people who gave at least one negative response on the customer satisfaction questionnaire. The control chart indicates that several points lie outside the control points. This could indicate that an event (assignable cause) occurred during the week in which those points fell outside the UCL. Perhaps during those weeks new staff members were being trained on the job or some employees resigned, leaving the bank understaffed. If we can identify assignable causes for these points, we should exclude these samples when calculating the control limits and center line. We do this because the control limits and center line are calculated to reflect how the process typically functions. If no assignable causes are apparent, then the current control limits and center line are appropriate.

The c chart

The p chart allowed us to display the percentage of customers who gave at least one negative response. We may, however, want to get an indication of how many negative responses there were among a given sample of customers. A customer may have many negative responses about the service he/she received. The c chart is a way of graphing this type of data, where c is the total number of negative responses indicated by the customers. The formula for the UCL, center line, and LCL are:

$$UCL = \bar{c} + 3\sqrt{\bar{c}}$$
$$\text{Center line} = \bar{c}$$
$$LCL = \bar{c} - 3\sqrt{\bar{c}}$$

where c is the number of negative responses per sample.

Sample	Number of Customers Who Gave at Least One Negative Response (D_i)	Percentage of Customers Who Gave at Least One Negative Response (p_i)
1	5	.10
2	20	.40
3	15	.30
4	16	.32
5	10	.20
6	8	.16
7	15	.30
8	20	.40
9	7	.14
10	2	.04
11	10	.20
12	13	.26
13	20	.40
14	13	.26
15	4	.08
16	4	.08
17	9	.18
18	11	.22
19	5	.10
20	6	.12
	total = 213	$\bar{p}$ = .213

TABLE 5.2 Data for the p control chart example (note $n = 50$)

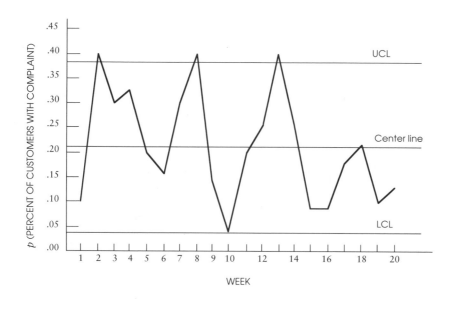

FIGURE 5.8 The *p* control chart using data from Table 5.2

Example of the *c* chart

I will use the banking example again to illustrate the *c* chart. We would now like to monitor the total number of negative responses from customers. We collect data for 20 weeks (see Table 5.3). After examining the data, we decide to create a control chart. The control limits and the center line are calculated to be:

$$UCL = 31.61$$
$$Center\ line = 18.65$$
$$LCL = 5.69$$

The *c* control chart is presented in Figure 5.9. The figure demonstrates that no points fall outside the control limits, suggesting that the process is in control. This indicates that the average number of negative responses per sample is approximately 19. Even though the process is in statistical control, the data indicate a high number of negative responses from customers. Changing this situation warrants a change in the banking personnel's contact with customers. This type of process change requires action from management and might include additional training for banking personnel, providing more tellers, or increasing the number of banking windows.

Additional data presented in Table 5.3 illustrate other methods of control charting based on the original information for the c control chart. The two additional variables, u and $p(tot)$, are calculated from c. The u variable reflects the average number of negative responses per person and is calculated by dividing c by the number of customers per sample. For our example, the variable u will be calculated by dividing c by 50. We can also plot this variable in a control chart called the u-chart. The formulae for the control limits and the center line are:

Sample (Week)	Number of Negative Responses (c_i)	Average Number of Negative Responses Per Person (u_i)	Percentage of Negative Responses out of all Possible Responses ($p_i(tot)$)
1	15	.30	.023
2	20	.40	.038
3	14	.28	.022
4	25	.50	.038
5	24	.48	.037
6	18	.36	.028
7	26	.52	.040
8	28	.56	.043
9	15	.30	.023
10	8	.16	.012
11	17	.34	.026
12	20	.40	.038
13	28	.56	.043
14	21	.42	.032
15	13	.26	.020
16	16	.32	.025
17	18	.36	.028
18	22	.44	.034
19	10	.20	.015
20	15	.30	.023
	$\bar{c} = 18.65$	$\bar{u} = .373$	$\bar{p}(tot) = .029$

TABLE 5.3 Data for the c control chart example (note $n = 50$)

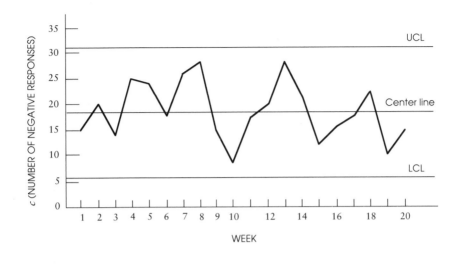

FIGURE 5.9 The c control chart using data from Table 5.3

$$UCL = \bar{u} + 3\sqrt{\frac{\bar{u}}{n}}$$

Center line $= \bar{u}$

$$LCL = \bar{u} - 3\sqrt{\frac{\bar{u}}{n}}$$

where u is the average number of negative responses per person for a given sample and n is the number of customers per sample.

Also, $p(tot)$ reflects the percent of negative responses out of all the possible responses for a given sample. Since our questionnaire had 13 questions, we calculate $p(tot)$ by dividing u by 13. Again, the $p(tot)$ variable can be incorporated into a control chart with its corresponding control limits and center line. The formulae are:

$$\text{UCL} = \bar{p}(tot) + 3\sqrt{\frac{\bar{p}(tot)(1-\bar{p}(tot))}{n(tot)}}$$

$$\text{Center line} = \bar{p}(tot)$$

$$\text{UCL} = \bar{p}(tot) - 3\sqrt{\frac{\bar{p}(tot)(1-\bar{p}(tot))}{n(tot)}}$$

where $p(tot)$ represents the percentage of negative responses for a given sample and $n(tot)$ represents the total possible number of responses for a given sample ($n(tot)$ = number of items * sample size).

It is important to note that the variables c and u might be misinterpreted, either indicating a product/service problem which does not actually exist or indicating no problem when a problem actually exists. It should be apparent that the number of negative responses from customers depends on the number of items on the questionnaire. A high number of questionnaire items creates a greater potential for negative responses.

For example, c (the number of negative responses) may equal 40 for a sample of 50 people responding to a 100-item questionnaire, while c equals 20 for a sample of 50 people responding to a 2-item questionnaire. By using the c chart or u chart, we might conclude that customers from the first sample are more dissatisfied than customers from the second sample, since the number of negative responses is larger in the first sample. A closer look indicates that this conclusion is not warranted.

We should look at the number of possible responses that could have been made by the sample. For the first sample, 5000 negative responses are possible (100 items * 50 customers). For the second sample, 100 negative responses are possible (2 items * 50 customers). In the first sample, negative responses constitute .8 percent of all possible responses, while in the second sample negative responses make up 20 percent of all possible responses.

Therefore, when using the c and u chart, we must consider the number of items on the questionnaire when making conclusions. One way to avoid this problem is to use the $p(tot)$ chart, since it takes into account the number of items on the questionnaire.

Summary

Customer satisfaction questionnaires can provide attribute data which we can subsequently incorporate into control charts for attribute data.

There are several types of control charts used with attribute type data. The p chart monitors the percentage of customers who give at least one negative response to the customer satisfaction questionnaire. The c chart monitors the total number of negative responses. From the c chart data, we can calculate other statistics (u and $p(tot)$) with corresponding control charts. Although we can apply data from customer satisfaction questionnaires to attribute control charts, the data is probably best suited for variable control charts.

CONTROL CHARTS FOR VARIABLE DATA

Recall that variable data represents measurements of quality characteristics. We can develop customer satisfaction questionnaires which provide scores reflecting units of measurement: the higher the score, the higher the quality of the service or product.

Because variable data is quantified in units of measurement, the distribution of scores can be represented by two statistics, the average and the standard deviation. The average represents the center of the distribution, and the standard deviation represents the variability of scores around the average. The larger the standard deviation, the wider the variability. In quality improvement efforts, it is customary to control both the average of the quality characteristics and the variability. Control of the average is accomplished with a control chart for means, the $\bar{x}$ chart. Control of the variability of the process can be accomplished with a control chart for the standard deviation, the s chart.

The $\bar{x}$ and s control charts

The $\bar{x}$ chart plots the means of a quality characteristic for each sample, while the s chart plots the standard deviations of the quality characteristic for each sample. For a given sample, we calculate the mean of the quality characteristic by adding the scores for the quality characteristic and dividing by the sample size, n. The formula for sample average was presented earlier. If we have a sample that consists of three observations where $x_1 = 5$, $x_2 = 4$, and $x_3 = 2$, then the mean for this sample equals:

$$\bar{x} = (5 + 4 + 2)/3 = 3.67$$

We can also calculate the average value of the sample averages. If we have a number of samples, it is possible to calculate averages for each sample and obtain an average of the sample averages. The formula for this overall average is:

$$\bar{\bar{x}} = \frac{\bar{x}_1 + \bar{x}_2 + \ldots + \bar{x}_m}{m}$$

where m equals the number of samples.

This overall sample average provides the center line for the control chart. Also, recall that the distribution for each of the samples can be represented by an index of variability called the sample standard deviation. To calculate the standard deviation, we will first calculate the sample variance. The formula for the sample variance was presented earlier in the chapter. After calculating the sample variance, we can calculate the standard deviation by taking the square root of this variance. Again, if we have multiple samples, we can calculate a sample standard deviation for each sample.

We can now calculate the average standard deviation for all the samples. This formula is:

$$\bar{s} = \frac{1}{m}\Sigma s_i$$

where m equals the number of samples, and Σs_i is the sum of all sample standard deviations.

We calculate the upper and lower control limits for the $\bar{x}$ chart using the average standard deviation. The calculation of the control limits also involves a constant, c_4, that depends on the sample size. A full explanation of this constant is presented in Montgomery (1985) and will not be discussed here. The upper and lower control limits for the s chart also depend upon two constants, B_4 and B_3, respectively. These constants are also discussed in Montgomery (1985).

Knowing the sample averages and the average standard deviation, we can now calculate the parameters for the $\bar{x}$ chart. The formulae for the center line and upper and lower control limits are:

$$UCL = \bar{\bar{x}} + \frac{3\bar{s}}{c_4\sqrt{n}}$$

$$\text{Center line} = \bar{\bar{x}}$$

$$LCL = \bar{\bar{x}} - \frac{3\bar{s}}{c_4\sqrt{n}}$$

where n equals the sample size.

Sample	Score for *Speed of Transaction* Dimension (Average of Items 3 and 4)	Sample Standard Deviation for *Speed of Transaction* Dimension
1	2.5	1.20
2	3.0	1.10
3	3.4	1.15
4	3.2	1.22
5	3.7	1.10
6	3.0	1.00
7	2.7	1.21
8	3.2	1.15
9	3.2	1.10
10	3.4	1.20
11	3.0	1.25
12	2.9	1.18
13	2.8	1.20
14	3.1	1.15
15	3.6	1.18
16	3.2	1.23
17	2.9	1.20
18	2.9	1.17
19	2.4	1.21
20	2.5	1.20
	total = 60.6	total = 23.4

TABLE 5.4 Data for the $\bar{x}$ and s control chart example (note $n = 25$)

The formulae for the parameters of the s chart are:

$$\text{UCL} = B_4 \bar{s}$$
$$\text{Center line} = \bar{s}$$
$$\text{LCL} = B_3 \bar{s}$$

Example of $\bar{x}$ and s charts

A bank would like to determine its customers' level of satisfaction. The bank collects data over 20 weeks using the customer satisfaction questionnaire in Figure 5.3. Each week the bank collects data from 25 customers. The bank decides that, of the four quality characteristics, the most important is the *speed of transaction* dimension (items 3 and 4). As a result, the bank examines only this dimension. The data appear in Table 5.4.

The center line and the upper and lower control limits for the $\bar{x}$ chart are:

$$UCL = 3.739$$
$$\text{Center line} = 3.03$$
$$LCL = 2.321$$

where the constant for the UCL and LCL are $c_4 = .9896$.

The center line and the upper and lower control limits for the s chart are:

$$UCL = 1.679$$
$$\text{Center line} = 1.17$$
$$LCL = 0.661$$

where the constants for the UCL and LCL are $B_4 = 1.435$ and $B_3 = .565$.

The control charts appear in Figure 5.10.

These two control charts indicate that the process is in statistical control. The $\bar{x}$ chart, however, indicates that there is considerable room for improvement. Since the scores can range from 1 to 5, the average score of 3.03 indicates that customers' perception of the quality of *speed of transaction* can be improved. Management intervention in the process will improve the average.

Once management implements changes, we can calculate differences between pre- and post-interventions and conduct statistical tests to see if these differences are substantial. The mathematical formula for testing differences in data is available in various statistics textbooks (Loftus and Loftus, 1988).

Charting and presenting the data can provide a feedback mechanism for employees who are in direct contact with the customers and who may directly influence customers' perceptions. Charting techniques such as these have been effective in increasing organizational productivity (Prichard, et al., 1988). In addition, goal setting, used in conjunction with this feedback method, can increase performance even more (Locke, et al., 1981).

ORGANIZATIONAL COMPARISONS

Not only can customer satisfaction data be used to make comparisons within a single organization across time; it can also be used to make

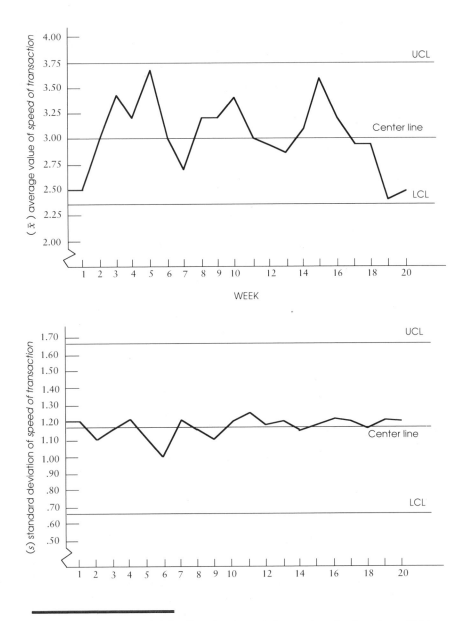

FIGURE 5.10 The $\bar{x}$ and s control chart using the data from Table 5.4

comparisons between organizations (see Appendices F through I). Comparisons between organizations can help identify areas for improvement for organizations with lower satisfaction scores on certain dimensions. An organization can determine dimensions on which it is poorly serving its customers and determine how other companies serve their customers on that particular dimension.

Organizations can also compare satisfaction with products. For example, some automobile manufacturers are designing their cars to make the driver "feel" better. A direct comparison between these cars and other cars could determine if these automobiles do, in fact, make the driver feel better. In fact, the comparison could use the customer satisfaction questionnaire in Figure 5.4.

Organizations making comparisons with other organizations would be taking some risk, since their scores may indicate that they are the lowest among all organizations in the comparison. However, the Malcolm Baldrige National Quality Award dictates that companies make these comparisons. With this type of data, organizations that score low will identify the dimensions on which they should focus their resources. Better organizational decisions based on actual data will allow these organizations to make improvements in appropriate areas.

DETERMINE EFFECTIVENESS OF INTERVENTION PROGRAMS

Companies spend millions of dollars on intervention programs designed to increase the quality of their services and products. Intervention often takes the form of formal employee training programs as well as new business processes to facilitate work flow. In either case, customer satisfaction questionnaires can determine the effectiveness of these programs (see Appendices F through I).

Training programs

Companies implement employee training programs to enable employees to fulfill their job duties. A company might have determined through a customer satisfaction questionnaire that its customers are not satisfied with the service they received. The company might, therefore, implement a program to improve employees' communication and interpersonal skills in hopes that this will lead to better employee-customer interactions.

The company might determine the effectiveness of such a training program by comparing customer satisfaction results before and after training. If customer satisfaction scores are higher after training than before, this provides evidence of the program's effectiveness. Statistical analyses will determine if differences are meaningful. There are various methods for determining the effectiveness of intervention programs (Campbell and Stanley, 1966).

Benchmarking

Benchmarking is the search for an industry's best practices that lead to excellent performance. Camp (1989) outlined a process of benchmarking which includes identifying premier companies and determining their business practices. Once a company identifies these superior business practices, it may incorporate them into its own practices or change existing processes to conform to the ones identified. This change is designed to increase the organization's effectiveness in meeting its customers' requirements.

It is important to determine if these changes have, in fact, led to increases in performance. Customer satisfaction questionnaires can index the effectiveness of this benchmarking process in changing customers' perceptions. This is done by examining the difference between customer satisfaction before and after benchmarking has been implemented.

ADDITIONAL QUESTIONS

Other questions might also be included in a customer satisfaction questionnaire. Some could solicit information about the time the customer received the service. This might reveal if differences in customer perception are due to factors present only at certain times of the day. A question about the location of the service might provide useful information. For instance, a bank could determine if certain branches are better than others at satisfying customers. Once identified, successful business processes from one location can be adopted by another. Also, a question asking for information on the type of product might determine if certain products are more appealing than others.

Additional questions could be included to obtain more information for comparisons. Companies should carefully choose questions that represent variables which would provide potentially rich information. Questions should have a specified purpose. If certain patterns are suspected (differences between branches, time of day, etc.), an additional question could help substantiate such predictions and lead to insights about possible improvements.

SUMMARY

The utility of customer satisfaction questionnaires is dependent, in part, on the use of the data. This chapter covered effective presentation of data. It also demonstrated other uses for customer satisfaction questionnaires: determining the quality dimensions of the product or service that strongly predict overall customer satisfaction, monitoring business processes over time, making organizational comparisons, and determining effectiveness of intervention programs. Figure 5.11 summarizes these uses.

CONCLUSIONS

This book presents practical guidelines to follow when developing customer satisfaction questionnaires. Chapters focused on the steps in the general model of customer satisfaction questionnaire development and use.

Chapter 2 discussed methods of determining customer requirements or quality dimensions. Customers judge services and products according to these dimensions. It is important to identify a comprehensive list of these quality dimensions, because they determine the content of the questionnaire. If a customer requirement is not identified in this first step, the questionnaire will be unable to assess an important element.

Developing and evaluating the questionnaire presents another important step in understanding customer attitudes. In Chapter 3, measurement issues highlighted the importance of reliability and validity of scales. Reliability is especially important when scores summarize or represent a quality dimension. Chapter 4 presented various rating formats used to quantify the quality of the service or product. Depending on the expected use of the data, either a checklist or rating scale may be appropriate. A checklist format is useful for providing attribute data; a rating scale provides variable data. Chapter 4 also included characteristics of good items, as well as information that should be included in the introduction of the questionnaire.

Customer satisfaction questionnaires have many applications (Chapter 5). They can monitor ongoing business processes, highlight general strengths and weaknesses, evaluate intervention programs, and help determine the most important customer requirements.

Use of customer satisfaction questionnaires will likely increase in the near future. Companies want to distinguish themselves from other com-

USES	IMPORTANT ISSUES
1. Present current standing of customer satisfaction.	■ Present means and standard deviations of specific items as well as overall scores of each dimension
2. Identify important customer requirements.	■ Use correlational analysis relating customer requirements to overall satisfaction scores
3. Monitor satisfaction levels over time.	■ Use control charting techniques
	■ Control chart method depends on type of response format you select (checklist–attribute data vs. Likert-type–variable data)
	■ Types of control charts include p chart, c chart, u chart, $\bar{x}$ chart, and s chart
4. Provide organizational comparisons.	■ Comparisons should be made on companies using same questionnaire
	■ Independent research firm could conduct comparisons
5. Determine program effectiveness.	■ Evaluate effect of training programs
	■ Conduct benchmarking studies

FIGURE 5.11 Uses of customer satisfaction questionnaires

panies in their ability to satisfy customers. Also, the Malcolm Baldrige National Quality Award places a strong emphasis on customer satisfaction. A company's ability to use customer-related information depends on the quality of the measurement system. The measurement system is often represented by customer satisfaction questionnaires designed to assess various dimensions of service or product quality. If information obtained from questionnaires is to be useful, questionnaires should reflect reliable and valid information. I hope this book has provided users of customer satisfaction questionnaires with useful guidance for developing and using these instruments.

INTRODUCTION
TO APPENDICES

In today's business, there is an increasing use of data in aiding the decision-making process. To understand data and how it can help in decision-making, we need to summarize and interpret the data. The remaining appendices provide a basic foundation for the interpretation of data, including specific examples using data resulting from questionnaires and other business processes and general examples.

A basic understanding of statistics is desirable but not necessary to grasp the fundamental principles that will be presented. The appendices are not intended to make the reader proficient in these statistical techniques. Many textbooks cover these topics, and the interested reader may consult the bibliography to learn more about these techniques. Although formulae for calculating various statistical indices are presented in this text, these statistical procedures usually require the assistance of a computer and appropriate statistical software because hand calculations are not practical with large data sets. The text presents formulae to allow you to see how these indices are, in fact, calculated. A final note: in some situations, you should consult an expert on these statistical techniques. Expert judgment is often necessary for interpreting statistical results.

The topics of the appendices fall into two major sections. The first (covered in appendices C through F) deals with descriptive statistics and sampling distributions. Specifically, Appendix C introduces the measurement process and presents four levels of measurement often used in data collection. Appendix D discusses frequency as a way of summarizing data, and also covers probability and distributions. Appendix E introduces measures of central tendency and variability as a means of summarizing data. Appendix F introduces one of the most important topics in the use of data in decision-making, sampling error. The reader must thoroughly understand this topic to appreciate subsequent appendices.

The second section of topics deals with the use of data in hypothesis testing. Appendix G covers decision-making and hypothesis testing. It outlines the elements involved in making a decision and formally presents the concept of hypothesis testing, including the types of errors that may occur in any decision-making situation. Appendix H introduces the t-test procedure, which allows us to examine the difference between two groups of numbers. Appendix I presents the analysis of variance procedure (ANOVA), which helps us examine the difference between two or more groups of numbers. Appendix J introduces the topic of correlational analysis, a procedure for summarizing the linear relationship between two variables. This chapter will include a discussion on the regression equation for a straight line. Appendix K discusses the use of factor analysis. This appendix provides only a brief introduction to a powerful technique in questionnaire development.

CRITICAL INCIDENTS INTERVIEW FORMS

Interview #_____ for critical incidents

Positive examples

1.
2.
3.
4.
5.
6.
7.
8.
9.
10.

Negative examples

1.
2.
3.
4.
5.
6.
7.
8.
9.
10.

SATISFACTION ITEMS AND CUSTOMER REQUIREMENT FORMS

Satisfaction item #1:

Critical incidents:

Satisfaction Item #2:

Critical incidents:

Satisfaction Item #3:

Critical incidents:

Customer Requirement #1:

Satisfaction items:
1.
2.
3.
4.
5.
6.
7.
8.

Customer Requirement #2:

Satisfaction items:
1.
2.
3.
4.
5.
6.
7.
8.

Customer Requirement #3:

Satisfaction items:
1.
2.
3.
4.
5.
6.
7.
8.

Appendix C

MEASUREMENT SCALES

Measurement scales are the means by which we assign a number to an object or entity. The number on the scale represents some characteristics of that object or entity. Stevens (1951) divided measurement scales into four types: nominal, ordinal, interval, and ratio. The degree to which these scales differ is reflected in the degree to which arithmetic operations make sense with the values of the entity represented by the numbers on the scale. The discussion of each scale will clarify this.

NOMINAL SCALE

A nominal scale categorizes objects. These objects are mutually exclusive, and the numbers on the nominal scale only reflect that the objects are different from one another. For example, we might use a nominal scale to categorize customers on the basis of their marital status:

> Single people are assigned a 1.
> Married people are assigned a 2.
> Divorced people are assigned a 3.

We may also use a nominal scale to label a set of stores:

> Bob's Barn is assigned a 1.
> Tom's Tent is assigned a 2.
> Stephen's Store is assigned a 3.
> Marissa's Mall is assigned a 4.

Let's look at arithmetic operations using the scale values for customers' marital status. Some operations that would *not* make sense are addition and subtraction. For example, a Stephen's Store (3) minus a Tom's Tent (2) would not equal a Bob's Barn (1). The only arithmetic operations that can be used on a nominal scale are the equality and inequality operations. For example, within our present store categorization system, a

Stephen's Store (3) is the same as another Stephen's Store (3). Also 1 ≠ 2 indicates that a Bob's Barn is not the same as a Tom's Tent.

Because the values on the nominal scale represent categories, they can also be identified by different symbols, such as letters of the alphabet. For example, a Bob's Barn might be labeled an "A," a Tom's Tent as "B," a Stephen's Store as "C," and a Marissa's Mall as "D."

ORDINAL SCALE

An ordinal scale uses numbers to order objects with respect to some characteristic. For example, we can place customers in order according to their satisfaction level. If person A is more satisfied than person B, and person B is more satisfied than person C, then person A is more satisfied than person C. Using an ordinal scale, we may assign a number to each of these people and rank them from least satisfied (person C) to most satisfied (person A). The numbers corresponding to this *satisfaction* ordinal scale could be:

> Person C is a 1.
> Person B is a 2.
> Person A is a 3.

Let's look at some arithmetic operations applied to ordinal scales. Equality/inequality operations can be applied to ordinal scales. For example, in an equality/inequality operation, we can say that person C (1) is not equal to person A (3). We can also use the operations of less than (<) and greater than (>) on ordinal scales. Statements such as 3 > 2 and 1 < 3 make sense, indicating that person A is more satisfied than person B and person C is less satisfied than person A, respectively.

Another example of ordinal scales is reflected in the ranking of companies on some variable. For example, in studying a wide variety of companies, a research firm may assess the satisfaction level of its customers. In a final report, the research firm ranks the companies from highest to lowest in terms of their customers' overall satisfaction level. Suppose the study included five companies. The company with the highest average score on the customer satisfaction questionnaire would be ranked #5; the company with the second highest score would be ranked #4; and so forth:

> Company A is a 5.
> Company B is a 4.
> Company C is a 3.
> Company D is a 2.
> Company E is a 1.

Although ordinal scales allow us to order objects, they do not allow us to determine the distance between the objects with respect to the characteristic being measured. For the example of ranking customers in terms of *satisfaction*, we know the order of the people but do not know much more satisfied one person is relative to another. Also, ranking the companies does not tell us how much more satisfied company A's customers are compared to customers of other companies. This inability to determine differences between objects relates to the ordinal scale's lack of a unit of measurement.

INTERVAL SCALE

An interval scale orders things so that differences between scale values are equal, because the interval scale has a unit of measurement. One example is the Fahrenheit scale.

We can use more arithmetic operations with interval scale values. In addition to the equality/inequality and ordering operations, we can perform subtraction. For example, the difference between 50°F and 40°F equals the difference between 120°F and 110°F.

Attitude questionnaires are assumed to possess the features of an interval scale. If this assumption is true, we can perform useful arithmetic operations with the data from such questionnaires, which will aid in the interpretation of the data.

RATIO SCALE

A ratio scale is similar to the interval scale in that it possesses a unit of measurement. The ratio scale has one additional feature: a meaningful zero point. An example of a ratio scale is the measurement of length. All arithmetic operations are meaningful for the ratio scale. This includes equality/inequality, ordering, subtraction, addition, and division. Table C.1 summarizes the characteristics of measurement scales.

MEASUREMENT SCALES IN CUSTOMER SATISFACTION

Some of the measurement scales can be used in customer satisfaction questionnaires to categorize customers (nominal scale) and differentiate customers along some continuum (interval scale). Development of questionnaires to assess customers' perceptions and attitudes is based on the

FUNCTIONAL USES

		establish equality/ inequality	establish rank ordering	establish equal differences between scale points	establish zero point
	Nominal	yes	no	no	no
Scale Types	Ordinal	yes	yes	no	no
	Interval	yes	yes	yes	no
	Ratio	yes	yes	yes	yes

TABLE C.1 Types of measurement scales and the functional uses of each

notion that the scales possess features found in the interval scale. In addition, we imply the use of a scale when we rank companies on the basis of their quality (ordinal scale). The ranking of companies is best accompanied by evidence that the ranking reflects meaningful, statistically significant differences between companies (see Appendix F).

Appendix D

FREQUENCIES, PERCENTAGES, PROBABILITIES, HISTOGRAMS, AND DISTRIBUTIONS

Data can be overwhelming. Often we are confronted with large data sets consisting of hundreds of scores. We need a way of summarizing the data to make some sense of it. This appendix will discuss one way of summarizing large data sets with the use of frequencies and histograms.

FREQUENCIES

Table D.1 lists scores from a hypothetical study examining the level of customer satisfaction of a given company. The data set contains 48 scores, each representing one person's average score on the customer satisfaction questionnaire. Upon examination, we see that scores vary somewhat, ranging from a low of 1.4 to a high of 4.6. To gain a better understanding of the data, we need to summarize the scores in a simple format.

One way of summarizing data is to calculate the frequency of occurrence of a specific value, or how often that given value occurs in our data set. To calculate frequencies, we first rank the scores from lowest to highest (see Table D.2). After the ranking, we determine the frequency of occurrence of each value. We see that the value of 1.4 occurred only once. Therefore, 1.4 has a frequency of one. Likewise, the value of 2.5 has a frequency of four.

Although calculating frequencies for each specific value will help summarize the information, the amount of information can still be overwhelming. For example, with characteristics measured in small incre-

2.3	4.3	3.3	1.5
2.5	2.7	3.4	3.2
4.1	3.8	3.7	2.9
3.0	2.7	2.5	3.4
4.6	2.3	2.1	2.3
3.7	3.6	1.4	3.2
1.5	1.6	1.7	3.6
4.0	4.1	3.4	2.1
3.3	3.1	3.5	4.4
2.5	2.8	3.9	2.0
1.7	2.5	2.9	3.8
4.2	2.1	3.9	2.4

TABLE D.1 Hypothetical data set

1.4	2.3	3.1	3.7
1.5	2.4	3.2	3.8
1.5	2.5	3.2	3.8
1.6	2.5	3.3	3.9
1.7	2.5	3.3	3.9
1.7	2.5	3.4	4.0
2.0	2.7	3.4	4.1
2.1	2.7	3.4	4.1
2.1	2.8	3.5	4.2
2.1	2.9	3.6	4.3
2.3	2.9	3.6	4.4
2.3	3.0	3.7	4.6

TABLE D.2 Data from table D.1 ranked from smallest to largest

ments, we may obtain a lot of values, each occurring with little frequency. Calculating the frequency of each value might not be enough to simplify the data. Therefore, when calculating frequencies, we usually group values with similar scores into a particular class. Then we calculate frequencies for these class values.

CLASS INTERVALS

A class interval represents a range in which a set of values is included. Creating class intervals is a process of dividing the scores into specified equal intervals. Each class interval is defined by a lower bound and an upper bound. The lower bound represents the lowest possible score that can be included in the interval; the upper bound represents the highest possible score. Using the data set in Table D.2, we can create a class interval with the width of 0.4 to represent the scores. Starting with a lower bound of 1.0, the first class interval would include scores ranging from a low of 1.0 to a high of 1.4. The second class interval would include scores ranging from 1.5 to 1.9. The last class interval would include scores ranging from 4.5 to 4.9. Table D.3 presents these class intervals and the frequency of values that occur in the class.

We use arbitrary numbers to select class intervals and determine the width of each class interval. It has been shown that if continuous data is divided into intervals, you lose less information about the data by creating more intervals. A reasonable number of intervals is seven (Shaw, Huffman, and Haviland, 1987), although more intervals would result in less information loss.

PERCENTAGES

Another way of looking at the frequency of values is through the use of percentages. A percentage reflects the proportion of scores of a particular value. The percentage for a particular value is calculated by dividing the frequency of a given value by the total number of scores in the data set. For our data, we see that the percentage of people with scores of 2.5 to 2.9 is 18.8 percent (9/48), and the percentage of people with scores ranging from 4.0 to 4.9 is 14.6 percent (7/48). The total of the percentages for a given question should be 100 percent (given rounding errors).

The percentage is sometimes preferred to the frequency since it incorporates the total number of scores into its calculation. A frequency of 50 may not tell us all we want to know about the data. A frequency of 50 in one sample of scores may indicate a large percentage (e.g., when sample size is 60), while in another sample a frequency of 50 may indicate a minute percentage (e.g., when sample size is 1,000,000). Thus, before interpreting the magnitude of the frequency, we should be aware of the total sample size.

Class interval	Frequency	Percentage
1.0 to 1.4	1	2.1%
1.5 to 1.9	5	10.4%
2.0 to 2.4	8	16.7%
2.5 to 2.9	9	18.8%
3.0 to 3.4	9	18.8%
3.5 to 3.9	9	18.8%
4.0 to 4.4	6	12.5%
4.5 to 4.9	1	2.1%
Total	48	100.0%

TABLE D.3 Frequencies for the class variable

CONSTRUCTING FREQUENCY DISTRIBUTIONS OF THE INTERVALS

We can graphically represent the frequencies of the class intervals. The graph is formally called a histogram. The histogram aids in summarizing the data beyond the lone use of frequencies since it captures many pieces of information in a single picture. The histogram not only indicates the frequency of each value, but also roughly indicates the range of the data (lowest to highest value) and the shape of the distribution.

The histogram has two axes. The horizontal axis (sometimes referred to as the X axis or abscissa) represents the variable or class interval. The vertical axis (sometimes referred to as the Y axis or ordinate) represents the frequency for a variable or class interval.

The horizontal axis is scaled by the midpoint of each class interval. Therefore, for the data in Table D.3, the horizontal axis would be scaled by eight values, each value representing the midpoint of each class interval. The midpoints are 1.2, 1.7, 2.2, 2.7, 3.2, 3.7, 4.2, and 4.7. The histogram appears in Figure D.1.

The frequency table and the histogram are both useful tools for summarizing data. The frequency table reflects the frequency of occurrence of specific values or the frequency of values for a specific class interval. The histogram is a graphic illustration of the frequency table.

We can calculate frequencies for variables that are on any scale of measurement (nominal, ordinal, interval, and ratio). For example, a questionnaire could include various questions pertaining to satisfaction levels as well as questions asking for demographic information. The demographic portion could include questions pertaining to sex and age.

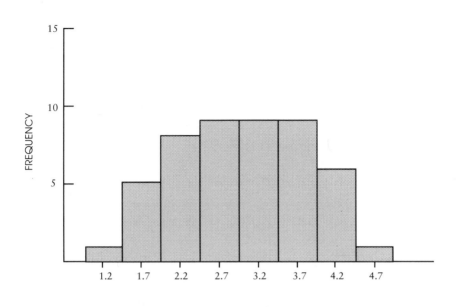

FIGURE D.1 Histogram of the class intervals in Table D.3

If the questionnaire was distributed to 150 people, we could subsequently calculate the frequency or proportion of males vs. females and also determine the frequency or proportion of a given age group.

The frequencies for the sex variable (nominal) and age variables (ratio) are listed in Table D.4. The frequencies indicate that the sample consists of more males than females. In terms of percentages, we see that males represented 58 percent (87/150) of respondents and females represented 42 percent of respondents. Also, this sample consists of a large group of people aged 36 to 45 years.

DISTRIBUTIONS

The histogram in Figure D.1 can also be called a distribution of scores. Although there are many forms of distributions, such as a bimodal (two-humped) distribution and a unimodal (one-humped) distribution, I will present a special type called a normal distribution. The normal distribution is a symmetric, bell-shaped distribution. Many of the things we measure in our environment can be described by a symmetric, bell-

Sex	Frequency	%	Age	Frequency	. %
M	87	58.0	0–15	0	0.0
F	63	42.0	16–25	3	2.0
			26–35	44	29.3
			36–45	64	42.7
			46–55	25	16.7
			56–older	44	9.3
Total	150	100.0%	Total	150	100.0%

TABLE D.4 Frequencies and percentages for the variables of sex and age

shaped distribution. For example, if the height of many people were plotted, the shape of the histogram would form a normal distribution.

DETERMINING PROBABILITIES FROM DISTRIBUTIONS

Given a distribution, we can calculate probabilities of various events. For example, we may have measured the height of 1,000 people. The data of height forms a normal distribution described by some mean and variance (see distribution of $n = 1$ in Figure F.1 on page 127). Now let's say we were to select one person at random from this sample. What is the probability that the height of that person is greater than 65"?

We determine the probability by dividing the number of people who are taller than 65" by the total number of people in the sample. We can also determine the probability by calculating the area under the curve to the right of 65". We can describe this area as a percentage of people who are taller than 65". We can then transform this percentage into a probability by dividing the value by 100.

As we increase the height of our criterion to 70", we see that the probability of selecting a person greater than that criterion decreases, since the area under the curve to the right of the criterion decreases.

SUMMARY

This appendix introduced various ways of describing and presenting data. Frequencies and percentages convey the occurrence of values in the data set. Histograms are a useful way of presenting data. They convey the frequency of values as well as the range of the data set. Histograms can also be thought of as distributions. The probability of a given event occurring can also be determined using the distribution.

DESCRIPTIVE STATISTICS

The use of frequencies and histograms is one way of summarizing data (see Appendix D). Another way to summarize large data sets is with the use of summary indices, which describe the shape of the histogram. Two types of summary indices help us understand the data: central tendency and variability.

CENTRAL TENDENCY

One way of summarizing data is to determine the center or middle point of scores. Measures of central tendency allow us to determine roughly the center of the scores in the data set. For example, we may measure the satisfaction level of 10 customers. The data are presented in Table E.1. The scores vary considerably. We can capture a lot of information about these scores by determining the middle point. By doing so, we get an estimate of where the scores fall. Three statistics that describe the central tendency are the mean, median, and mode.

MEAN

The mean is the arithmetic average of all scores in the data set. It is calculated by adding all the scores in the data set and dividing by the total number of observations in the data set. The formula is:

$$\bar{x} = \frac{\Sigma x_i}{n}$$

where n = the number of observations in the data set and Σx_i is the sum of all scores in the data sets.

Customer	X
1	4
2	1
3	3
4	2
5	4
6	1
7	5
8	4
9	3
10	2

TABLE E.1 Hypothetical data set

Score	Customer	X	
1	7	5	
2	1	4	
3	5	4	
4	8	4	
5	3	3	← $(n/2)$th score
6	9	3	← $(n/2 + 1)$th score
7	4	2	
8	10	2	The median is $(3 + 3)/2 = 3$
9	2	1	
10	6	1	

TABLE E.2 Hypothetical data set

Using the formula, we can calculate the mean of the data in Table E.1:

$$\bar{x} = \frac{4 + 1 + 3 + 2 + 4 + 1 + 5 + 4 + 3 + 2}{10} = 2.9$$

MEDIAN

Another measure of central tendency is the median. The median is the middlemost score after the data has been rank ordered from either highest to lowest or lowest to highest. In other words, half of the scores have values larger than the median and half have values smaller than the median. If the data set has an odd number of scores, the median is the (n + 1 / 2)th largest score in the data set. If the data set has an even number of scores, the median is the average of two numbers, the (n/2)th largest score and the (n/2 + 1)th largest score. Table E.2 provides the rank order of data from Table E.1. Since the number of scores in the data set is even, the median is calculated as the average of the two middlemost scores. The median value in the data set is 3.

MODE

The third measure of central tendency is the mode. The mode is the score that occurs most often in the data set. In Table E.2, there are two 1s, two 2s, two 3s, three 4s, and one 5. Therefore, the mode of this data set is 4, since it is the most frequently occurring score. It is possible that a data set could have more than one mode. This occurs when two or more values in the data set have the highest frequency and the same frequency.

VARIABILITY

While measures of central tendency indicate the middle of the distribution, we also would like to know about the spread of data. The spread of data is indexed by measures of variability. Measures of variability indicate the extent to which scores are tightly packed together vs. spread out. The measures of variability presented here are the variance and the standard deviation. Both measures indicate the spread of data around the mean.

VARIANCE

Table E.3 contains four columns of numbers. The first column is x, the score; the second column contains a deviation score from the mean ($x - \bar{x}$); the third column contains the squared deviation score; and the last column is the squared value of each score.

One measure of variability is the variance. Variance, s^2, is the sum of the squared deviations about the mean (SS) divided by the number of scores in the data set less one. The formula for the variance is:

$$s^2 = \frac{\sum(x_i - \bar{x})^2}{n - 1} = \frac{SS}{n - 1}$$

The numerator is the sum of the squared deviations about the mean (SS) and the denominator is called the degrees of freedom. In general, the degrees of freedom for a particular statistic is the number of observations in the data set minus the number of estimated parameters used in the equation. The total number of observations used in the calculation is the sample size (n), and the number of estimated parameters used in the equation is one (the sample mean). It should be noted that some people, in calculating the variance, divide the SS by n instead of n-1. Usually, n is used when the variance is used to describe the present data set, while n-1 is used to make inferences about the population variance from which the sample is drawn. A more complete discussion between the difference is available in various introductory statistics books. Using the equation above, the variance of the data is calculated:

$$s^2 = \frac{4 + 1 + 0 + 1 + 4}{4} = 2.5$$

The formula for the sum of squared deviations (SS) can be simplified to facilitate hand computation of the variance. The formula for the sum of squares is:

$$SS = \sum x_i^2 - \frac{(\sum x_i)^2}{n}$$

x	$x - \bar{x}$	$(x - \bar{x})^2$	x^2
1	−2	4	1
2	−1	1	4
3	0	0	9
4	1	1	16
5	2	4	25
Totals 15	0	10	55

TABLE E.3 Deviation scores and squared deviation scores for hypothetical data

Using the data, the SS is calculated to be:

$$SS = 55 - \frac{225}{5} = 10$$

The numerator for the formula of the variance is the squared deviation of each score from the mean. As the scores are widely spread out from the mean, the numerator increases. Therefore a large variance indicates that the scores are widely spread out, and a small variance indicates that the scores are tightly packed around the mean.

STANDARD DEVIATION

Another measure of variability is the standard deviation. The standard deviation is simply the square root of the variance and is denoted by s. The standard deviation for the data in Table E.3 is calculated to be $s = 1.58$. The larger the standard deviation, the larger the spread in the data.

If the data are normally distributed, the standard deviation can be used to estimate the percentage of scores that fall within a specified range. By definition, 68 percent of the scores fall within a range whose limits are (mean − 1s) and (mean + 1s), and 95 percent of the scores fall within a range whose limits are (mean − 2s) and (mean + 2s). If the standard deviation is small, a high percentage of the data falls closely around the mean. For our data, approximately 68 percent of the data falls within a range from 1.4 to 4.4.

SUMMARY

This section included measures of central tendency and measures of variability. Both types of measures summarize information contained in a sample of scores. The central tendency measures determine the score in the data set around which all other scores cluster. Measures of variability determine the extent of spread of the data.

Appendix F

STATISTICS, PARAMETERS, AND SAMPLING DISTRIBUTIONS

A subset of observations can be randomly selected from a larger set of observations. The larger set of observations is called the population; the smaller set is called the sample. We are usually concerned with making conclusions about the population. Since the population can be extremely large, we often examine a sample to make conclusions about the larger population. For example, we may want to know the level of satisfaction of all our customers. Due to limited resources, we may only be able to measure the satisfaction level of a small set of customers. The population consists of all the customers; the sample consists of the small set of customers we measure.

We may examine the mean and the variance of a sample to make inferences about the mean and variance of the population. Numbers calculated from a sample of data are referred to as *statistics*. Therefore, the mean, variance, and standard deviation of the sample are statistics. Numbers calculated using the entire population are called *parameters*. Statistics are denoted with the following symbols: the mean is $\bar{x}$, the variance is s^2, and the standard deviation is s. Parameters are usually denoted with Greek symbols: the population mean is μ, the variance is σ^2, and the standard deviation is σ. Because the population parameters may not be easily obtained (due to limited resources), we have to estimate the parameters. We use the statistics as estimators of the parameters.

SAMPLING ERROR

Suppose we have a population of 1,000 people and want to make conclusions about their mean height. We may have only the resources to measure 50 of these people. We use the mean from the sample to estimate the mean of the population.

For the sake of argument, suppose we knew the mean height of the population to be $\mu = 60''$ with a $\sigma^2 = 50''$. Based on our sample of 50 randomly selected people, we calculate the mean of their height. Suppose we found the mean height of the sample to be $\bar{x}_1 = 62''$. Now, let's place this sample back into the population of 1,000 people and take another sample of 50 randomly selected people. Suppose we found the mean of this sample to equal $\bar{x}_2 = 55''$. We notice that there is some difference between the means of the first and second sample of people, both differing from the true population mean.

The difference of the sample means from population mean is referred to as *sampling error*. This error is expected to occur and is considered to be random. For the first sample, we happen to select, by chance, people who were slightly taller than the population mean. In the second sample, we selected, again by chance, people who were slightly shorter than the population mean.

STANDARD ERROR OF THE MEAN

In the preceding example, we witnessed the effect of sampling error; in one sample the mean $(\bar{x}_1) = 62''$ and in the second sample the mean $(\bar{x}_2) = 55''$. If we did not know the population mean (which is usually the situation), we could not determine the exact amount of error associated with any one given sample. We can, however, determine the degree of error we might expect using a given sample size. We could do so by repeatedly taking a sample of 50 randomly selected people from the population, with replacement, and calculating the mean for each sample. Each mean would be an estimate of the population mean.

If we collected 100 means, we could then plot them to form a histogram or distribution. This distribution is described by a mean and a standard deviation. This distribution of sample means is called a *sampling distribution*. The mean of this sampling distribution would be our best estimate of the population mean. The standard deviation of the sampling distribution is called the standard error of the mean (sem). The sem describes the degree of error we would expect in our sample mean. If the population standard deviation is known, we can calculate the sem. The standard error of the mean can be calculated easily using the following formula:

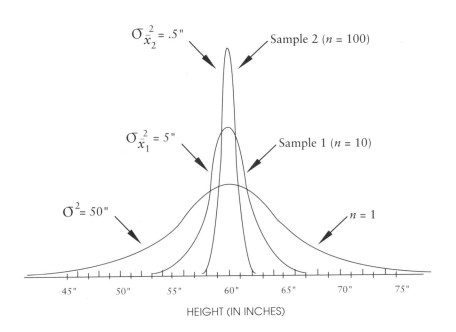

FIGURE F.1 Sampling distributions for sample sizes of $n = 100$ and $n = 10$ with a population mean of 60 and population variance of 50

$$\text{standard error of the mean} = \frac{\sigma}{\sqrt{n}}$$

where n is sample size and σ is the population standard deviation. If we do not know the population standard deviation, we can calculate the sem using the sample standard deviation as an estimate of the population standard deviation.

The sampling distributions for two different sample sizes are presented in Figure F.1. The population mean (μ) is 60″ and the population variance (σ^2) is 50″. The size of sample 1 is 10 and the size of sample 2 is 100. Using the equation above, the standard error of the mean is 2.24″ for sample 1 and 0.71″ for sample 2. As seen in Figure F.1, the degree of sampling error is small when the sample size is large. This figure illustrates the effect of sample size on our confidence in the sample estimate.

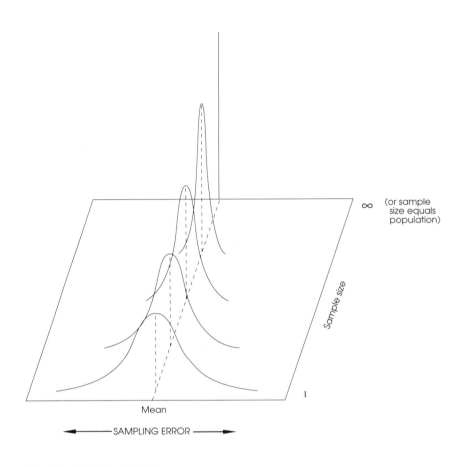

FIGURE F.2 The relationship between sample size and sampling error: as sample size increases, sampling error decreases

When the sample size is 100, we see that any one of our sample means will likely fall close to the population mean (95 percent of the sample means will fall within the range of 58.58″ to 61.42″). When the sample size is ten, our sample means will deviate more from the population mean than do our sample means when using a sample size of 100 (95 percent of the sample means will fall within the range of 53.68″ to 66.32″). In fact, when the sample size equals the population size, the standard error of the mean is 0. That is, when sample size equals population size, the sample mean will always equal the population mean.

Figure F.2 illustrates the relationship between sampling error and sample size. As sample size increases, sampling error decreases. When sample size equals one, the standard error of the mean is by definition the standard deviation of the observation. When sample size equals the size of the population, there is no error in ·the estimate of the population mean. Thus, the standard error of the mean is 0 when sample size equals the size of the population.

SUMMARY

Statistics are numbers derived from a sample of numbers. Parameters are numbers derived from a population. A sampling distribution is a distribution of a given statistic. Sampling error describes the degree of error associated with a given statistic for a specified sample size. As sample size increases, sampling error decreases. The concept of sampling error can be applied to many statistics (mean, t value), and the concept of sampling error will be applied throughout the remaining appendices.

DECISION MAKING AND HYPOTHESIS TESTING

Decisions are made every day in the business world. On a small scale, we decide whether or not to leave early for a meeting being held on the other side of town. On a larger scale, companies select one supplier over another. We implicitly make decisions about some aspect of the world. In the former scenario, we might decide to leave early if the roads are icy and we need extra time to get to the meeting. In the second scenario, a company might select one supplier over another because one supplier makes parts of higher quality.

When we make decisions, we hope they are correct. A decision is correct if it is congruent with the state of the world. For example, a decision to leave early for the meeting is correct if the roads are icy and incorrect if the roads are not icy. In addition, a decision not to leave early for the meeting is correct if the roads are not icy and incorrect if the roads are icy.

REALITY AND DECISIONS

One morning, you are deciding whether or not to take your umbrella to work. To help you make this decision, you rely on some evidence (data). This evidence consists of several weather forecasts from various sources, each providing you with some data on the weather for the day. You must decide, based on this data, whether or not to take your umbrella with you.

You can make one of two choices based on your evaluation of the data. If you decide the data indicate it will rain today, you will take your umbrella. If you decide the data indicate it will not rain today, you will leave your umbrella at home.

There are four possible outcomes for this scenario. We can diagram these, crossing the two states of the world with the two possible deci-

State of the World

		No Rain	Rain
Carry Umbrella		Error (Type I)	Correct Decision
Your Decision			
Do not Carry Umbrella		Correct Decision	Error (Type II)

FIGURE G.1 Four possible outcomes, crossing the two states of the world with the two decisions

sions. The two states of the world constitute reality—the way the world truly is. The two decisions are based on the evaluation of the evidence (data), leading us to decide whether or not an umbrella is warranted. The diagram depicting the four possible outcomes is presented in Figure G.1 and illustrates the two correct decisions and the two types of errors. For the sake of discussion, I labeled the errors as Type I and Type II.

THE PROCESS OF DECISION-MAKING

We can look at decision-making as a process consisting of two important elements: the evidence and the criterion. The evidence is the data we evaluate in making our decision. In our previous umbrella-toting example, we may have gathered data from many local weather reports, the Farmer's Almanac, and other sources. The criterion reflects the amount of evidence or data we need to decide whether to carry an umbrella. Therefore, differences in our criterion will influence the likelihood of making a Type I versus a Type II error. We could have a stringent criterion, which means we need a lot of evidence to convince ourselves to carry an umbrella (e.g., we will carry an umbrella only when all of the forecasts predict rain). With this stringent criterion, we will rarely end up carrying an umbrella on a day without rain (not likely to make a Type I error), but will likely end up not carrying an umbrella on a rainy day (likely to make a Type II error). On the other hand, we could have a lenient criterion, which means we need little evidence to convince us to carry an umbrella (e.g., we will carry an umbrella if at least one forecast predicts rain). With this criterion, we would likely carry an umbrella on a day which there is no rain (likely to make a Type I error), but we will rarely end up without an umbrella on a rainy day (not likely to make a Type II error).

DECISION MAKING IN HYPOTHESIS TESTING

In business, we would like to know the real state of the world. To understand the true state of the world, we collect data. The data constitute the evidence we need to make conclusions about the world. Based on this evidence, we decide which state of the world is true.

Let's look at an example to illustrate the role of decision-making in hypothesis testing. We may own two stores and have limited financial resources. We would like to give resources to the store that needs the most help (has the lowest level of customer satisfaction). We develop a customer satisfaction questionnaire and administer it to the stores' customers. Questionnaire scores constitute the data we need to make conclusions about the state of the world.

We can formally state our question: Do the two groups of customers have different levels of satisfaction? In hypothesis testing, we set up the world as consisting of two mutually exclusive hypotheses: the null hypothesis and the alternative hypothesis. The null hypothesis (H_o) states:

> There is no difference in satisfaction levels between the customers of the two stores.

The alternative hypothesis (H_A) states:

> There is a difference in the satisfaction levels between the customers of the two stores.

In the world, only one of these hypotheses is true. In our study, we will collect evidence to help us decide which is correct. In our hypothesis testing situation, we have a possibility of four outcomes. We have two possible states of the world crossed with two possible decisions. Each state of the world is represented by one of our hypotheses (there is no difference vs. there is a difference). We also have two decisions we can make (deciding there is a difference between the two stores or that there is not a difference between the two stores). These decisions are unique to hypothesis testing. Formally, we state our decisions as either rejecting the null hypothesis (or accepting the alternative hypothesis that there is a difference between the two stores) or not rejecting the null hypothesis (not accepting the alternative).

State of the World

		Null hypothesis true	Alternative hypothesis true
	Reject null hypothesis	Type I error (α)	Correct decision $(1 - \beta)$
Your Decision			
	Do not reject null hypothesis	Correct decision $(1 - \alpha)$	Type II error (β)

FIGURE G.2 The four possible outcomes in a hypothesis testing situation, crossing the two states of the world with the two decisions

We can construct a decision outcome matrix for this situation. This is presented in Figure G.2. The four cells, similar to the four cells in our umbrella-toting situation, can be characterized by probabilities, or likelihoods of occurrence. The probability of rejecting the null when the null is, in fact, true (upper left corner) is labeled as α. The probability of not rejecting the null when the null is true is $1 - \alpha$. In addition, the probability of failing to reject the null when the alternative is true is labeled as β. The probability of rejecting the null when the alternative is true is $1 - \beta$.

SOME EVIDENCE

We need to collect data to provide us with evidence of the true state of the world. Let's use our example concerning the level of satisfaction of customers from our two stores. We collect data from two samples, each representing one store. Higher scores on the questionnaire reflect higher levels of satisfaction. The data are presented in Table G.1.

Before examining the data, let's discuss the kind of evidence that would indicate whether or not we should reject the null. If the null is correct, then the two groups of scores should be roughly the same. If the alternative is true, then the two groups of scores should be different; one set should contain higher scores than the other.

We need a way of summarizing the data to allow us to decide which hypothesis is true. In this situation, we could look at the overall average of each group. The average score for Store 1 is $\bar{x}_1 = 3.5$, and the average for Store 2 is $\bar{x}_2 = 3.1$. The difference between these two scores is 0.4. We could use this difference score as the summary score. This summary score reflects the degree of difference between the two groups and is, essentially, the evidence.

DETERMINATION OF THE CRITERION

Summary scores are used to represent the state of the world, supporting either the null hypothesis or the alternative hypothesis. We need a criterion to judge whether the summary score reflects that the null hypothesis is true or that the alternative hypothesis is true. In hypothesis testing, we usually set the criterion to reflect that the alpha level (probability of rejecting the null when it is true) equal .05. That is, given that the null is true, we want to set a criterion with which we will incorrectly reject the null hypothesis, at the most, five times out of 100.

For our study, we found that the summary score (the difference between the two groups), is 0.4. Recall that in Appendix F, the effect of sampling error would result in differences between two samples of scores even if the samples were selected from the same underlying population. Therefore, the difference of 0.4 revealed in our study might not indicate

Store 1	Store 2
4	3
5	4
2	3
4	4
5	2
4	2
3	3
4	5
2	2
2	3

TABLE G.1 Hypothetical data of satisfaction scores for two stores

1. Generate null and alternative hypothesis:
   ▪ null is: there is no difference
   ▪ alternative is: there is a difference

2. Collect data to provide evidence of the state of the world.

3. Using the data, determine the summary score which summarizes the difference between the groups.

4. Determine criterion to which to compare your summary score.

5. Decide to reject the null or not reject the null.

TABLE G.2 Steps in hypothesis testing

any real difference at all. The difference between the two samples could be due to sampling error.

For our example, the criterion we choose should reflect a difference between two samples that would occur by chance only five times out of 100 if the null were true. This criterion is established through formal methods discussed in the next three appendices.

SUMMARY

Hypothesis testing involves determining the extent to which the differences between our samples is not likely due to sampling error. When the difference is likely due to sampling error, we do not reject the null hypothesis; the two samples are likely from the same population. When the difference is not likely due to sampling error (difference is large), then we reject the null hypothesis in favor of the alternative hypothesis.

The steps to hypothesis testing are presented in Table G.2. The first step is to generate a null and an alternative hypothesis. The second step is to collect data to provide evidence of the state of the world (supporting the null or alternative hypothesis). The third step is determining a summary score using data that reflect the difference between the groups. The fourth step is determining the criterion, reflecting the point at which the summary score is likely to occur five times out of 100 if the null hypothesis is true. Fifth, if the summary score exceeds the criterion, we reject the null hypothesis and accept the alternate hypothesis.

Appendix H

T-TESTS

We may want to compare two groups of people on some variable. Two companies in the retail business have a friendly competition with each other. In fact, Bob of Bob's Barn claims that his customers are highly satisfied, while Tom, owner of Tom's Tent, claims he has more satisfied customers. Both owners would like to obtain empirical information to determine which company has the highest level of customer satisfaction.

An independent research firm was contacted to see if it could settle the score. The research firm developed a customer satisfaction questionnaire to assess overall customer satisfaction. Higher scores on the questionnaire reflect higher satisfaction. This questionnaire was administered to two sets of customers. One set had received service from Bob's Barn and the other from Tom's Tent. The research firm obtained 20 customers from each company to complete the questionnaire. The data appear in Table H.1.

The mean for the group from Bob's Barn is 2.85, and the mean for the group from Tom's Tent is 3.45. If we only inspect these mean values, we might conclude that customers from Tom's Tent are more satisfied with service than customers from Bob's Barn.

Recall that when two small sets of data are compared, their means will almost always be different from each other, even if the two data sets come from the same population. This difference is due to sampling error (see Appendix F). This error arises because the observed mean is only an estimate of the population mean, which has inherent error because it is based on only a sample of data. Therefore, merely seeing if there is a difference between the two groups is not enough to say that the two data sets arise from two different populations.

The *t*-test provides a method by which we can more rigorously compare two data sets. Conducting a *t*-test informs us whether the degree of difference between the two data sets could be due to factors other than sampling error. If the results indicate that the difference between the groups is not likely due to sampling error, we believe that the two data sets probably do not come from the same population.

CALCULATION

The formulae for the calculation of the t-test vary, depending on whether the sample sizes for each group are equal. The general equation presented below can be applied to situations in which the sample sizes are either equal or not equal. The calculation of the t-test is:

$$t\,(N-2) = \frac{\bar{x}_1 - \bar{x}_2}{\sqrt{\left(\dfrac{SS_1 + SS_2}{n_1 + n_2 - 2}\right)\left(\dfrac{1}{n_1} + \dfrac{1}{n_2}\right)}}$$

where $\bar{x}_1$ and $\bar{x}_2$ are the means for each group, SS_1 and SS_2 are the sum of squares for each group, n_1 and n_2 are the sample sizes for each group, and N is the sum of n_1 and n_2.

Also, $(N-2)$, associated with the t statistic, is the degrees of freedom. Recall that the degrees of freedom is the total number of observations (N) minus the number of estimated parameters. Using the data in Table H.1, the observed t value is calculated to be:

Bob's Barn		Tom's Tent	
1	3	2	3
2	4	4	3
3	3	5	4
2	2	3	5
4	1	3	3
3	3	4	2
3	4	2	1
3	2	5	3
4	4	4	4
4	2	5	4

Total $=$	57.00	69.00
$n\ =$	20	20
$\bar{x}\ =$	2.85	3.45
$SS\ =$	18.55	24.95

TABLE H.1 Hypothetical data for two companies

$$t(38) = \frac{3.45 - 2.85}{.338} = 1.77$$

If we assume that the null hypothesis is true (there is no difference between the two groups), we would expect the t statistic to equal 0.0 (since $\bar{x}_1 - \bar{x}_2 = 0$). The t statistic, like the sample mean, can also be described by a sampling distribution with associated sampling error. That is, *even though the null might be true*, we would not expect to obtain a t statistic of zero every time we randomly sampled two samples from the same population. Given that the null hypothesis is true, the mean of the t distribution is symmetric around zero. If we were to randomly sample t values from this distribution, we would likely see a majority of t values clustering around 0. We would not likely see extreme t values. Recall that 95 percent of the data falls within 2 standard deviations above or below zero. If the t value we obtain from our study is more than $2s$ away from the mean, we know this finding is highly unlikely; therefore, we think the two sample means do not come from the same population.

When the t values are extreme, we think the two samples come from different populations (reject the null hypothesis and accept the alternative hypothesis). We say the two sample means are *statistically significantly* different from each other. In significance testing, we set a critical value which our observed t value should exceed if we are to say the means are significantly different from each other. This critical t value is determined to be the t value above which the probability of obtaining a t value, by chance, is .05.

The spread of the t distribution is determined by the sample size used in the calculation of the t statistic. The spread of the t distribution is wider when sample size is small, and becomes narrower as the sample size increases. A given t distribution (with associated degrees of freedom) describes the frequency with which we would see varying t values if we repeatedly performed independent t-tests with a given sample of subjects (20 in each group). For our example we would be interested in the probability of obtaining t values using a t distribution with 38 degrees of freedom.

The observed t value we obtain in our study is 1.77. We compare this t value to a critical t value. The critical t value at the 5 percent level (with 38 degrees of freedom and a two-tailed test) is $t = 2.02$. This critical t value represents the point above which our chance of obtaining an obtained t value is less than 5 percent if the null hypothesis were true. Our observed t value is below this critical t value. Thus, we conclude that the difference between our observed means (2.85 and 3.45) is likely due to sampling error, or that both sets of customers come from one underlying population; the customers from Bob's Barn and Tom's Tent are equally satisfied.

FACTORS AFFECTING SIGNIFICANCE TESTING

Power is the probability of finding a significant difference with our samples when there truly is a difference between the two populations. We always strive to have a high degree of power when we conduct significance testing. One way of increasing power is by increasing the sample size on which the t-test is conducted. Another is to use scales with high reliability. In our example, perhaps customers from Tom's Tent were more satisfied but our test lacked sufficient power to detect this difference.

SUMMARY

The t-test can determine if the difference between two samples is meaningful. We calculate the observed t value using our data and compare it to a critical t value. This critical t value is the cut-off point above which the probability of obtaining a t value is .05. If our observed t is greater than this critical t value, then we say the difference between the two means is not likely due to sampling error. That is, the data likely come from two different populations. On the other hand, if the observed t value falls below the critical t value, we say the observed difference between the two means is likely due to sampling error. That is, the data from the two groups likely come from the same population and the observed difference is the result of chance. The power of detecting true differences can be increased by increasing the sample size on which the t-test is conducted and also by using measures with high reliability.

Appendix I

ANALYSIS OF VARIANCE

Analysis of Variance (ANOVA) is used to compare groups. When conducting an ANOVA, we can compare more than two groups simultaneously. As the name of the analysis implies, analysis of variance is a method of analyzing components of variance.

Let's look at an example. Suppose we have four independent sets of data. The data are presented in Table I.1. We will calculate the variance of the observations with two methods. The first method is to calculate the variability within each group. Four separate variances, one for each group, can be calculated. These four separate variances are each an estimate of the same variance. Therefore, we can get an overall variance measure by averaging these four variances. This average variance is the pooled variance estimate (s^2_p). This approach results in a variance estimate of .625.

The second method is to calculate the variance of the means (s^2_x). The variance of the means, however, is dependent on the sample size (see Appendix F). As sample size increases, the variance of the means decreases. Thus, to correct for sample size, we multiply the variance of the means by the sample size for each group $(n = 10)$. This estimate now reflects the variabilty of the group means corrected for sample size (ns^2_x). This approach results in a variance estimate of 7.49.

If there is no true difference between the group means, then the two variance measures should be roughly the same. We see, however, that the variability using the group means approach is 7.49, and the variance using the within-group approach is .625. The magnitude of the former variance indicates that there is considerable variability between groups, more so than variability within groups. In ANOVA, we are comparing these variance components. If the variance calculated using the means is larger than the variance calculated using individual scores within groups, this might indicate that there is a significant difference between the groups.

	Set 1	Set 2	Set 3	Set 4
	2	4	2	3
	1	5	3	2
	2	5	1	3
	1	4	4	2
	2	4	3	4
	2	4	3	3
	2	5	4	4
	3	3	3	2
	3	4	3	3
	2	3	2	4
Mean =	2.0	4.1	2.8	3.0
n =	10	10	10	10

$$SS_1 = 3.996 \qquad SS_2 = 4.896 \qquad SS_3 = 7.596 \qquad SS_4 = 6.003$$

$$s^2_1 = .444 \qquad s^2_2 = .544 \qquad s^2_3 = .844 \qquad s^2_4 = .667$$

$$s^2_p = (s^2_1 + s^2_2 + s^2_3 + s^2_4)/4 = .625$$

$$SS_B = 20.0^2 + 41.0^2 + 28.0^2 + 30.0^2 - (20 + 41 + 28 + 30)^2/4 = 6.741$$

$$s^2_{\bar{x}} = SS_B/3 = .749$$

TABLE I.1 Hypothetical data of four groups

CALCULATIONS

The standard method for presenting the results of the ANOVA is the tabular format. The ANOVA table appears in Table I.2. The first row of the ANOVA table contains information about the variance of the groups. The second row contains information concerning the variance of the subjects within each group. The third row of the table represents total variance. Each of the rows contains specific information about the variability of its respective components.

The first column identifies the sources of variation. The differences between groups is denoted by Between (B). The variation due to subjects within each group is denoted by Within (W). The total variation is denoted by Total. The second column in the ANOVA table represents the sum of squared deviations (SS). The SS_B and the SS_w should sum to SS_{TOT}. The third column represents the degrees of freedom for each SS. The degrees of freedom (df) for SS_B are the number of groups minus one. The degrees of freedom for SS_W are the total sample size minus the number of groups. The degrees of freedom for SS_{TOT} are the total sample size minus one. The df_B and the df_W should sum to df_{TOT}. The fourth column, mean square, represents the measure of variation of a particular source. The mean squares are calculated by dividing the sum of squares by the degrees of freedom. The last column represents the ratio of the MS_B to the MS_W and is referred to as the F ratio.

TESTING

The F value is a ratio of the variance of the means corrected for by sample size to variance within the groups. A large F value indicates that the between-group variance is larger than the within-group variance. Like the t statistic, the F value can also be described by a distribution, the F distribution. The F distribution has two different degrees of freedom, one associated with the estimate of the variance of the means $(k - 1)$ and the other associated with the variance within groups $(N - k)$. The exact shape of the distribution is determined by the df_B and df_W.

The concept of testing in ANOVA is the same as the testing using the t test. We compare the observed F value from our study to a critical F value. This critical F value is a cutoff point, above which the probability of obtaining an F value is only .05 if the null hypothesis is true. Therefore, an observed F value above the critical value, because it is such an unlikely event, would lead us to believe that the different groups in our study do not come from the same population.

Source	Sum of squares	Degrees of freedom (df)	Mean square	$F(df_B, df_W)$
Between	SS_B	$k - 1$	$SS_B/(k - 1)$	MSB
Within	SS_W	$N - k$	$SS_W/(N - k)$	MSW
Total	SS_{TOT}	$N - 1$		

Note: N = total sample size, k = number of groups, df = degrees of freedom

TABLE I.2 Analysis of Variance (ANOVA) table

The ANOVA table for the data in Table I.1 is presented in Table I.3. We see that the resulting F value is large. The critical F value with 3 and 36 degrees of freedom is approximately equal to 2.9. Our observed F value equals 11.99, which is larger than the critical F. Thus, we conclude that all four groups do not come from the same underlying population; at least one group comes from a different population from the rest.

POST-HOC COMPARISONS

When we compare three or more groups and find a significant effect using the ANOVA method, we can only conclude that the group means are significantly different from each other. Unlike the t-test, in which only two groups are compared, the ANOVA method can be inconclusive. For example, if we find the t-test to be statistically significant, we examine the means of the two groups to see which group is higher. In the ANOVA with three or more groups, a significant F-test only tells us that the groups do not come from the same population. In other words, significant effect indicates that there is at least one statistically significant difference between two of the groups in our study. Some of the groups may not be significantly different from each other, while others might be significantly different.

Source	Sum of squares	Degrees of freedom	Mean square	F(3, 36)
Group	22.475	3	7.492	11.987
Within	22.5	36	.625	$p = .0001$
Total	44.975	39		

Note: p = the probability of our observed F value occurring by chance.

TABLE I.3 Analysis of Variance (ANOVA) table for the data in Table I.1

To determine where the underlying differences lie, we must do further testing, referred to as post-hoc testing. There are various methods of post-hoc testing. All are somewhat related to the t-test method in which individual groups are compared to determine if they are significantly different from each other. The reader is referred to the bibliography to learn more about these techniques.

Appendix J

REGRESSION ANALYSIS

To understand the application of regression analysis, let's first look at an example of the relationship between two variables: 1) a person's level of satisfaction with perceived quality of service received from a company in terms of availability; and 2) the person's level of overall satisfaction with service. Perceived quality of availability is defined as the extent to which the customer perceives the company as being available to provide service whenever he/she needs it. Overall satisfaction with the service is defined as the extent to which the customer is generally satisfied with the way he/she was treated by the company. Measures were developed to assess both variables on a five-point scale. A higher number on either scale represents better service.

We use these measures on a sample of 10 people and subsequently obtain two scores: X_i, which represents perceived quality of availability, and Y_i, which represents overall satisfaction. The data is presented in Table J.1. The first column in the table provides the names of 10 people who were given the questionnaire. The second and third columns present the scores on *perceived availability* and *overall satisfaction*, respectively, for each of the 10 people.

A graphic representation called a scatterplot indicates the relationship between these two variables. This is seen in Figure J.1. As one would expect, there is a positive relationship between these two variables. That is, customers who perceive the company as more available to provide services when needed, have higher levels of satisfaction. The relationship can be summarized by a line, a regression line, which indicates the degree of relationship between X and Y. This relationship can also be described by an equation:

$$Y = a + bX + e$$

where b and a are constants representing the slope and intercept of the regression line, respectively. The error associated with the prediction is labeled as e.

The intercept is the predicted score for Y when X is equal to zero, the point at which the line intersects the Y axis. The slope represents the change in Y given a unit change in X. The values of a and b describe the regression line. Different values of each will necessarily lead to different regression lines. For a given relationship between two variables, there is a regression line that best fits the scatterplot. The parameters, a and b, for the best-fitting regression line are calculated by the following equations. The formula for b is:

$$b = \frac{n\sum X_i Y_i - (\sum X_i)(\sum Y_i)}{n\sum X_i^2 - (\sum X_i)^2}$$

We use b to calculate a:

$$a = \frac{\sum Y_i - b\sum X_i}{n}$$

These two equations are used to calculate the best fitting regression line. For the data in Table J.1, the regression slope is calculated to be:

$$b = .756$$

and the intercept is calculated to be:

$$a = .782$$

Customer	Xi	Yi	$(Xi)^2$	$(Yi)^2$	$XiYi$
Lance A.	3	5	9	25	15
Curt C.	1	2	1	4	2
Brian F.	3	3	9	9	9
Joe F.	5	4	25	16	20
Deanna F.	2	1	4	1	2
Lamona F.	2	2	4	4	4
Bob H.	4	4	16	16	16
Tom H.	3	4	9	16	12
Sandro I.	1	1	1	1	1
Scott M.	4	3	16	9	12

$$\sum Xi = 28 \quad \sum Yi = 29 \quad \sum Xi^2 = 94 \quad \sum Yi^2 = 101 \quad \sum XiYi = 93$$

$$r = \frac{10(93) - (28)(29)}{\sqrt{[10(94) - (28)^2][10(101) - (29)^2]}} = .726$$

TABLE J.1 Hypothetical data for variables X and Y

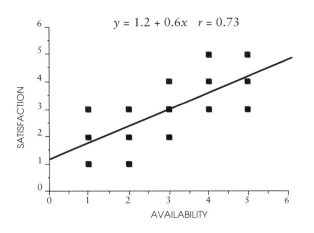

FIGURE J.1 A scatterplot representing the relationship between perceived availability and overall satisfaction with service

Therefore, the regression equation for predicting Y (overall satisfaction) from X (perceived availability) is:

$$Y = .782 + .76X$$

This equation can be used to make predictions of Y for any given level of X. If a person had an X score of 4.5, their predicted score for Y would be 4.2. If a person had an X score of 1.25, their predicted score for Y would be 1.73.

DETERMINING THE DEGREE OF FIT

An important step in regression analysis is to determine how well the regression line represents the data. That is, we want to determine how well the regression line fit the data. We determine this fit with an index called Pearson r^2. This index varies from 0 to 1.0. This index approaches 1.0 as the data lie closely near the regression line. The index approaches 0 as the data are widely dispersed around the regression line. The formula for the Pearson r^2 is:

$$r^2 = \frac{[n\sum X_i Y_i - \sum X_i \sum Y_i]^2}{[n\sum X_i^2 - (\sum X_i)^2][n\sum Y_i^2 - (\sum Y_i)^2]}$$

This index can be interpreted as the percentage of variance in Y (the criterion) that is accounted for by X (the predictor). So, if r^2 is equal to .70, we say that 70 percent of the variance in Y is accounted for by differences in X. Conversely, we could also say that 30 percent of the variance in Y is not accounted for by differences in X (this is essentially the variance that is unexplained by the X variable). The r^2 for data presented in Table J.1 is calculated to be:

$$r^2 = \frac{[10(93) - (28)(29)]^2}{[10(94) - (28)^2][10(101) - (29)^2]} = .528$$

The r^2 indicates that about 53 percent of the variance in Y is accounted for by differences in X.

PEARSON r

The r^2 is an index that describes how well the data fit a straight line. However, the r^2 does not tell us the direction of the relationship between the two variables. The linear relationship between two variables can be indexed by a single number, the Pearson correlation coefficient, denoted by the letter r. The Pearson r indicates the strength and direction of relationship between two variables. It can vary from -1 (a perfectly negative relationship between two variables) to 1 (a perfectly positive relationship between two variables). A negative relationship indicates that as one variable increases, the other variable decreases. A positive relationship indicates that as one variable increases, the other variable also increases.

The equation for the Pearson r is:

$$r = \frac{n\Sigma X_i Y_i - \Sigma X_i \Sigma Y_i}{\sqrt{[n\Sigma X_i^2 - (\Sigma X_i)^2][n\Sigma Y_i^2 - (\Sigma Y_i)^2]}}$$

Table J.1 includes data on two variables, X and Y. Using the equation above, we determine the extent to which variables X and Y are related to each other. The direction of their relationship is positive, and the strength of their relationship is $r = .73$. The amount of variance in Y accounted for by X (r^2) is calculated by squaring the correlation coefficient ($r^2 = .73^2 = .53$).

Figure J.2 illustrates various strengths and directions of relationships. A high correlation (either positive — Figure J.2(a) — or negative — Figure J.2(b)) indicates that there is a substantial relationship between the two variables. Figures J.2(c) and (d) indicate that there is a moderate relationship between the two variables. In fact, we know, by the size of the

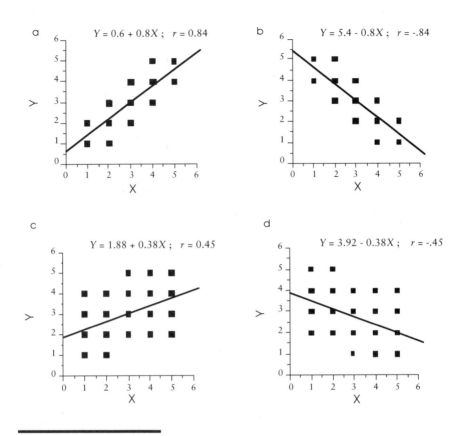

FIGURE J.2 Scatterplots indicating various strengths and directions of relationships between two variables

correlation coefficient, that the relationship between X and Y is stronger in the two former figures. For example, the two variables in Figure J.2 (a) have a positive correlation of .84, while the two variables in Figure J.2(c) have a moderate positive correlation of .45.

TESTING SIGNIFICANCE OF FIT

We test the significance of the r by first transforming the r statistic to a t statistic. The formula for the transformation is:

$$t(n - 2) = \frac{r\sqrt{n - 2}}{\sqrt{1 - r^2}}$$

We can calculate the t from the r in our present example. In our example $n = 10$ and

$$t(8) = \frac{.73\sqrt{8}}{\sqrt{1 - .53}} = 3.01$$

We can determine if the t represents a significant effect (see Appendix H).

SUMMARY

The relationship between two variables can be described by a straight line, a regression line. The regression line allows us to predict values of Y (with a degree of error) from given values of X. The degree of fit of data around the regression line is indexed by the correlation coefficient, denoted by r. It is an index of the linear association between the two variables. The correlation coefficient can range from -1 (perfect negative relationship) to 1 (perfect positive relationship). A correlation of zero indicates no linear relationship between two variables.

The next appendix covers another procedure that extends the concept of correlational analysis. This procedure, factor analysis, determines the relationship between observed variables and hypothetical variables.

Appendix K

FACTOR ANALYSIS

Factor analysis is a general term used to refer to a number of statistical techniques that can be used in questionnaire development. There are several types of factor analysis methods, each with its own particular method for generating results. Even though each of these methods is different, they often result in the same conclusions regarding interpretation of the data. Therefore, the present discussion will be very general and will not focus on one particular method of factor analysis but will instead describe the general factor analytic technique.

Generally, factor analysis is used when you have a large number of variables in your data set and would like to reduce the number of variables to a manageable size. For example, the 12 items presented in Table K.1 might be used to assess service quality of a particular organization. You might think that they represent 12 dimensions of customers' attitudes, but upon inspection, we see that they might not really represent 12 different dimensions.

For example, items 1, 2, and 3 are similar to each other and might be represented by a broader dimension called *availability* of the provider. In addition, items 4, 5, and 6 might represent *responsiveness* of the provider, and items 7, 8, and 9 represent *professionalism*. Items 10, 11, and 12 represent *overall satisfaction* with the service.

Let's say that we had a large number of people complete the questionnaire. A factor analysis of the resulting data would tell us whether there is a smaller set of more general dimensions (like *availability* and *responsiveness*). We reduce the original number of variables to a smaller number of dimensions so we can more easily interpret the information contained in the data. If we want to see the interrelationship (correlation coefficients) between these 12 variables, we would have to calculate and interpret 60 correlations. This may be difficult, since we are not able to understand what all of the interrelationships would indicate. By reducing the number of dimensions—say, reducing the 12 variables to the four dimensions suggested earlier—we now only have to calculate and interpret six relationships.

In general, factor analysis examines the relationships between a large set of variables and tries to explain these correlations using a smaller

1.   I could get an appointment with the merchant at a time I desired.
2.   The merchant was available to schedule me at a good time.
3.   My appointment was at a convenient time for me.
4.   The merchant was quick to respond when I arrived for my appointment.
5.   The merchant immediately helped me when I entered the premises.
6.   My appointment started promptly at the scheduled time.
7.   The merchant listened to my opinion about what I wanted.
8.   The merchant conducted herself/himself in a professional manner.
9.   The merchant was courteous.
10. The quality of the way the merchant treated me was high.
11. The way the merchant treated me met my expectations.
12. I am satisfied with the way the merchant treated me.

TABLE K.1 Customer opinion statements concerning service quality and overall satisfaction

number of variables. Initially, factor analysis uses the overall correlation matrix of the variables and determines which items share an underlying dimension. Factor analysis mathematically identifies the number of *factors* or underlying dimensions that best represents the observed correlations between the initial set of items. Generally, in the set of existing items, those that are highly correlated with each other will be represented by a single factor or dimension.

After the number of factors or dimensions has been identified, the next step in factor analysis is to determine which items fall within their respective dimensions. This is done by a mathematical procedure called *rotation*. This rotation will clarify the dimensions' relationships with the items. As with the general method of factor analysis, various methods of rotation exist. Generally, these different rotation methods result in the same conclusions regarding which dimensions represent a given set of items.

EXPLORATORY AND CONFIRMATORY USES OF FACTOR ANALYSIS

Factor analysis explores the possibility that our variables can be reduced to a smaller, undetermined number of factors. That is, we do not know the number of factors that represents our variables nor which variables load on which factors. Factor analysis, in this situation, will identify which variables load on their respective factors. Factor analysis can also be used in a confirmatory manner in which we go into the analysis with

	Factor		
Items	I	II	III
1.	.80	.05	.07
2.	.77	.04	.21
3.	.45	.11	.13
4.	.02	.55	.04
5.	.10	.77	.21
6.	.11	.88	.16
7.	.09	.08	.72
8.	.30	.21	.77
9.	.21	.22	.67

FIGURE K.1 A factor pattern matrix with the factor loadings from the results of a hypothetical factor analysis of the responses to nine items

some guess as to the outcome of the factor analysis (i.e., we think we know the number of factors and which variables load on which factors).[1] This use of factor analysis is guided more by hypothesis testing. We expect the results from the factor analysis to confirm our hypothesis of the variables in our data set. For example, if we develop a questionnaire designed to assess certain dimensions of service quality, we expect that the items on our scale represent their respective factor or dimension.

HYPOTHETICAL FACTOR ANALYSIS

The results of the factor analysis (the number of factors and factor rotation) are presented in a tabular format called a factor pattern matrix. The elements in the factor pattern matrix represent the regression coefficient (like a correlation coefficient) between each of the items and the factors. These elements indicate the degree of relationship between the variables and the factors.

Figure K.1 presents a hypothetical factor pattern matrix representing the results of a factor analysis which identified the existence of three

[1] The term *confirmatory factor analysis* is used here to illustrate how factor analysis can be used and is different from the more sophisticated approach of confirmatory factor analysis using significance testing.

factors that represented nine items. Items 1 through 3 have a high loading on factor I and small loadings on the other factors. Items 4 through 6 load highly on factor II, and items 7 through 9 load highly on factor III. A factor's definition is determined by the content of the items which load on it.

This hypothetical factor analysis indicates it would be reasonable to think of the data set as containing three variables rather than nine. Therefore, instead of looking at each variable as its own separate dimension, we would believe that there are 3 dimensions, each composed of three items. To obtain a score for each of the dimensions, we might combine the variables associated with a given factor to represent that dimension. That is, we would combine all the items that loaded highly on factor I to get a measure of that dimension. We would do the same for the items associated with factor II and factor III.

Now we would have three dimensions with which to work. These dimensions are useful summary variables for drawing conclusions about the data. Furthermore, we could now more easily interpret the interrelations (correlation coefficients) among these dimensions.

ACTUAL FACTOR ANALYSIS

This next example is taken from actual data obtained from a beauty salon using a customer satisfaction questionnaire. Although the questionnaire contained the items listed in Table K.1, I will only include items 1 through 6 in this example. The first three items were written to reflect an *availability* dimension, while the last three items were written to reflect a *responsiveness* dimension. I performed a method of factor analysis called principle factor analysis. This initial factor analysis resulted in the factor pattern matrix presented in Figure K.2.

As this factor pattern indicates, the factor analysis identified the existence of two factors or dimensions representing these six items. We expected this. However, it might be unclear as to which items represent factor 1 and which represent factor 2. All of the six items seem to load fairly high on factor 1. Factor 2 seems to reflect a bipolar scale: some items load positively on the factor, while others load negatively on the factor. The interpretation of the factor pattern matrix becomes even more difficult as the number of items and factors increases. To make the results of the factor analysis more meaningful, we use rotation.

On the initial factor pattern matrix, I conducted a method of rotation called varimax rotation. Other methods of rotation were used and, as expected, resulted in the same pattern of results as varimax rotation. Therefore, this presentation will only include the results of varimax rota-

Unrotated Factor Matrix

	Factor 1	Factor 2
Item 1	.727	.683
Item 2	.842	.425
Item 3	.321	.861
Item 4	.807	−.537
Item 5	.604	−.652
Item 6	.84	−.361

FIGURE K.2 The factor pattern matrix resulting from the factor analysis of six items designed to measure perceived availability and perceived responsiveness

Orthogonal Transformation Solution—Varimax

	Factor 1	Factor 2
Item 1	.14	.987
Item 2	.391	.858
Item 3	−.288	.873
Item 4	.966	.086
Item 5	.879	−.131
Item 6	.881	.244

FIGURE K.3 The result of the factor analysis after "rotating the factors"

tion. The rotated factor pattern matrix appears in Figure K.3. In this factor pattern matrix, the interpretation of the factors is more clear. Factor 1 is clearly represented by the last three items, while factor 2 is clearly represented by the first three items.

As expected, we found the existence of two factors that underlie these six items. In a sense, we used factor analysis to confirm our expectations. By design, the first three items reflected an *availability* dimension of service while the last three items reflected a *responsiveness* dimension. The factor analysis confirmed our hypothesis as to the number of factors that these six items represent, thus making us more confident that the items measure what they were designed to measure.

SUMMARY

Factor analysis identifies the number of underlying dimensions that account for the relationship between many items. Since factor analysis allows you to determine which items measure similar things, it is often used as a means of data reduction.

Bibliography

American Educational Research Association, American Psychological Association, and National Council on Measurement in Education. 1985. *Standards for Educational and Psychological Testing.* Washington, DC: American Psychological Association.

Anastasi, A. 1988. *Psychological Testing.* New York: Macmillan.

Brown, F. G. 1983. *Principles of Educational and Psychological Testing.* New York: Holt, Rinehart and Winston.

Camp, R. C. 1989. *Benchmarking: The Search for Industry Best Practices That Lead to Superior Performance.* Milwaukee, Wis.: Quality Press.

Campbell, D. T., and Fiske, D. W. 1959. Convergent and discriminant validation by the multitrait-multimethod matrix. *Psychological Bulletin* 56: 81–105.

Campbell, D. T., and Stanley, J. C. 1966. *Experimental and Quasi-Experimental Designs for Research.* Boston: Houghton Mifflin Co.

Chandler, C. H. 1989. Beyond customer satisfaction. *Quality Progress* 22(2):30–32.

Cottle, D. W. 1990. *Client-Centered Service: How to Keep Them Coming Back for More.* New York: John Wiley and Sons.

Cronbach, L. J. 1951. Coefficient alpha and the internal structure of tests. *Psychometrika* 16: 297–334.

Cronbach, L. J. 1984. *Essentials of Psychological Testing.* 4th ed. New York: Harper & Row.

Cronbach, L. J., and Meehl, P. E. 1955. Construct validity in psychological tests. *Psychological Bulletin* 52: 281–302.

Dawes, R. M. 1972. *Fundamentals of Attitude Measurement.* New York: John Wiley and Sons.

Edwards, A. L., and Kenney, K. C. 1946. A comparison of the Thurstone and Likert techniques of attitude scale construction. *Journal of Applied Psychology* 30:72–83.

Flanagan, J. C. 1954. The critical incident technique. *Psychological Bulletin* 51:327–358.

Fishbein, M. 1967. *Readings in Attitude Theory and Measurement.* New York: John Wiley and Sons.

Goodman, J. 1989. The nature of customer satisfaction. *Quality Progress* 22(2):37–40.

Guion, R. M. 1965. *Personnel Testing.* New York: McGraw-Hill.

Gulliksen, H. 1987. *Theory of Mental Tests.* Hillsdale, New Jersey: Lawrence Erlbaum Associates, Publishers.

Guttman, L. L. 1950. The basis for scalogram analysis. Vol. 4 of Stouffer, S. A.; Guttman, L.; Shuchman, E. A.; Lazarfeld, P. W.; Star, S. A. and Clausen, J. A. (eds.) *Studies in Social Psychology—World War II.* Princeton, N.J.: Princeton University Press.

Hannan, M., and Karp, P. 1989. *Customer Satisfaction: How to Maximize, Measure, and Market Your Company's "Ultimate Product."* New York: American Management Association.

Kennedy, D. A., and Young, B. J. 1989. Managing quality in staff areas. *Quality Progress* 22(10), 87–91.

Kenny, D. A. 1987. *Statistics for the Social and Behavioral Sciences.* 2d ed. Boston: Little, Brown and Co.

Latham, G. P., Fay, C.; and Saari, L. 1979. The development of behavioral observation scales for appraising the performance of foremen. *Personnel Psychology* 32:299–311.

Latham, G. P.; Saari, L.; and Fay, C. 1980. BOS, BES, and baloney: Raising Kane with Bernardin. *Personnel Psychology* 33:815–821.

Latham, G. P., and Wexley, K. N. 1977. Behavioral observation scales for performance appraisal purposes. *Personnel Psychology* 30:255–268.

Likert, R. A. 1932. Technique for the measurement of attitudes. *Archives of Psychology.* No. 140.

Lissitz, R. W., and Green, S. B. 1975. Effect of the number of scale points on reliability: A Monte Carlo approach. *Journal of Applied Psychology* 60:10–13.

Locke, E. A.; Shaw, K. N.; Saari, L. M.; and Latham, G. P. 1981. Goal setting and task performance: 1969–1980. *Psychological Bulletin* 90:125–152.

Loftus, G. R., and Loftus, E. F. 1988. *The Essence of Statistics.* 2d ed. New York: Alfred A. Knopf.

Montgomery, D. C. 1985. *Introduction to Statistical Quality Control.* New York: John Wiley & Sons.

Morrison, D. F. 1976. *Multivariate Statistical Methods* 2d ed. New York: McGraw-Hill.

Morrison, D. F. 1983. *Applied Linear Statistical Methods.* Englewood, N.J.: Prentice Hall.

Murine, G. E. 1988. Integrating software quality metrics with software QA. *Quality Progress* 21(11):38–43.

Neter, J.; Wasserman, W.; and Kutner, M. H. 1985. *Applied Linear Statistical Models* 2d ed. Homewood, Ill.: Richard D. Irwin, Inc.

Nunnally, J. M. 1978. *Psychometric Theory* 2d ed. New York: McGraw-Hill.

Parasurman, A.; Zeithaml, V. A.; and Berry, L. L. 1985. A conceptual model of service quality and its implications for future research. *Journal of Marketing* (fall):41–50.

Parasuraman, A.; Zeithaml, V. A.; and Berry, L. L. 1988. SERVQUAL: A multiple-item scale for measuring consumer perceptions of service quality. *Journal of Retailing* 64:12–40.

Pedhazur, E. J. 1982. *Multiple Regression in Behavioral Research: Explanation and Prediction* 2d ed. New York: Holt Rinehart Winston.

Pritchard, R. D.; Jones, S. D.; Roth, P. L.; Stuebing, K. K.; Ekeberg, S. E. 1988. Effects of group feedback, goal setting, and incentives on organizational productivity. *Journal of Applied Psychology* 73, 337–358.

Reckase, M. D. 1990. Scaling techniques. In Goldstein, G. and Herson, M. (eds.) *Handbook of Psychological Assessment*. New York: Pergamon Press.

Shaw, D. G.; Huffman, M. D.; and Haviland, M. G. 1987. Grouping continuous data in discrete intervals: information loss and recovery. *Journal of Educational Measurement* 24(2):167–173.

Society for Industrial and Organizational Psychology, Inc. 1987. *Principles for the Validation and Use of Personnel Selection Procedures*. 3d ed. College Park, Md.: Author.

Stevens, S. S. 1951. *Handbook of Experimental Psychology*. New York: John Wiley and Sons.

Thurstone, L. L. 1929. Theory of attitude measurement. *Psychological Bulletin* 36:224–241.

Zeithaml, V. A.; Parasuraman, A.; and Berry, L. L. 1990. *Delivering Quality Service: Balancing Customer Perceptions and Expectations*. New York: The Free Press.

Index